THE FATIMA CENTURY

HOW THE PILGRIM VIRGIN IS CHANGING OUR GENERATION

Thomas J. McKenna

*Catholic Action for Faith and Family is a lay organization
inspired by the teachings of the Roman Catholic Church and dedicated
to upholding and promoting the ideals of Christian Civilization.*

CATHOLIC ACTION
FOR FAITH AND FAMILY
SAN DIEGO

Published by Catholic Action for Faith and Family
P. O. Box 910308, San Diego, CA 92191
CatholicAction.org
Copyright 2017 by Thomas J. McKenna

Cover and interior design: Monika Stout
Midnight Book Factory, MidnightBookFactory.com

Printed in the United States of America
ISBN 978-0-9816314-5-5

Table of Contents

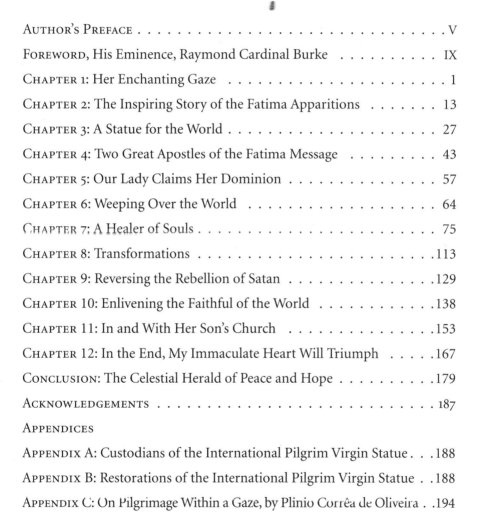

Author's Preface

*I*t is a singular privilege to write a book about a spiritual and religious phenomenon that has never been fully discussed in the history of literature. Mr. John Haffert, the renowned author, co-founder of the Blue Army, and creator of the International Pilgrim Virgin Statue, frequently suggested that I write a book about the Statue and its history, and anyone who knew Mr. Haffert when he was alive knows that it was hard to turn him down. I told him numerous times that I was more of a man of action than a writer, but he would not take no for an answer, and this book is the product of his holy insistence. Numerous times he said to me, "If you don't write it, Thomas, nobody will." With Mr. Haffert's determination in mind, and believing in the prophetic mission of this Statue, I began collecting information, researching, and conducting interviews, a process that has lasted over twenty years.

One experience in particular made me understand why Mr. Haffert was so intent on convincing me to take on this project. In the latter part of his life Mr. Haffert focused his prodigious energies on the formation of lay apostles. I was invited to speak at one of his Lay Apostolate Foundation conferences in the late Nineties and was given a graced insight into his passion for Our Lady as She manifests Her presence through the Statue. On the final night of the conference I stepped out of the closing banquet early to spend a few minutes in prayer with the Pilgrim Virgin. The Statue was beautifully displayed in a dimly-lit room nearby where a spotlight was focused on Her. When I arrived, Mr. Haffert was already there seated a few feet from the Statue. Apparently, independent of each other, we had both left the banquet early and found ourselves at the feet of Our Lady, just the two of us there in silence and prayer.

He didn't look at me when I entered the room but seemed to be aware of my presence. He continued to stare at the lovely face of Our Lady on the Statue and was obviously deep in prayer. "Isn't that gaze miraculous?" he suddenly said out loud as he looked over at me with a big smile on his face. He then looked back at Her attentively and continued to speak to me. "The visage of this Statue changes at different times and circumstances. I've never seen anything like it." Having been one of the Statue's Custodians for almost two decades then, I could only nod in affirmation and marvel at how deeply Mr. Haffert understood the transformative effect of that gaze. Here was the Statue's creator and greatest apostle, and he continued to be captivated by Our Lady's image even into his eighties. He could still sit before Her gaze with a sense of wonder and astonishment. "She is so maternal, so loving…" his voice trailed off. In prayer, before Our Lord, I understood John Haffert's passion as never before.

Although I have been unable to fulfill Mr. Haffert's wish for almost two decades, there came a time when the project seemed to beg for completion, and I must say that it has had an overwhelmingly positive effect on me. Reviewing the marvels of the Pilgrim Virgin Statue at close quarters for these many months, examining documents, reading associated materials and feedback, delving into the stories that surround this amazing gift of God, and especially recalling the special occasions when I traveled with the Statue, my faith in Jesus and my love for Our dear Lady have deepened immensely. I am very grateful for John Haffert's persistent request for this book!

In this book I intend to document some of the "marvels of grace" from seventy years of Our Lady's unrelenting pilgrimage through a sinful world, the signal graces of which are more evident than ever. I do not believe that anyone has yet provided a comprehensive account of the myriad blessings and transformations that have been effected due to the Pilgrim Virgin Statue's missionary presence in various parts of the world, so it is my privilege to offer documented and eye-witness accounts of these encounters. As will become evident in the course of this book, no one is left unaffected by Her presence, Her beauty, Her enchanting gaze. It is almost as if the Statue is a sacramental presence of the one great Sacrament of history, Christ Himself, who comes to men most effectively in Her through whom He first entered the world.

This simple Statue, from its very inauguration in 1947, has been given a special grace to change millions of lives. While many people have heard stories about favors or alleged miracles regarding the Statue – and I will address some of them in the book – I intend to focus, rather, on the singular fruit of the Statue's appearances which is really the most impressive miracle of all; namely, the sheer numbers of people who come to see the Statue and experience a conversion, a return to the Church, or a return to the life of grace through the Sacraments. A miracle doesn't have to be flashy or spectacular to be transformative. It's the normal miracles, if you will, that Our Lady uses most effectively to bring souls into the Kingdom of Christ. Seventy years of hindsight have made it evident that Her pilgrimage throughout the world in the ambassadorial guise of the Pilgrim Virgin Statue is nothing less than a vast quest for souls. I have seen many priests utterly amazed at the confession lines that inevitably form wherever the Pilgrim Virgin Statue passes. Priests have told me that they have not witnessed such an abundance of penitents in their confessionals in decades.

This is fundamentally a work of evangelization because it is a book about the preeminent Evangelizer of the world: the Mother of God. Through a series of apparitions in 1917, the Blessed Mother came to earth to warn us of the consequences of sin. Through another series of decisions and actions by dynamic personalities, She somehow brought into the world the Catholic sacramental known as the International Pilgrim Virgin Statue. The message and the Statue are inseparable, as are the graces and blessings that flow from taking the Fatima message to heart.

In the past thirty-five years (half of the time that the Statue has been in existence) I have been privileged to accompany the Queen in Her travels to various parts of the world, in Her mission of evangelizing souls, and it is my prayer that all who read this book will be filled with the same zeal of Our Lady of Fatima for the souls of every person on earth and the hope that we will all make our way to Heaven guided by the light of Her enchanting gaze.

Thomas J. McKenna
May 13, 2017
San Diego, California

Foreword

HIS EMINENCE,
RAYMOND CARDINAL BURKE

I first met Thomas McKenna shortly after my episcopal consecration in 1995. He was a regular observer at the meetings of the Conference of Bishops in the United States of America, and it was in the context of those meetings that I developed a friendship with him. Seeing that I was a new Bishop, he offered me help with various practical needs. In time, I came to know him more and more, and learned about his great zeal for the apostolate, inspired, most of all, by a deep devotion to Our Lady of Fatima and, therefore, by an even deeper devotion to the Most Blessed Sacrament and the Most Sacred Heart of Jesus. In 2006, he was inspired to found an apostolate, Catholic Action for Faith and Family, in order to do his part, with the help of divine grace and under the guidance and protection of Our Lady of Fatima, in the promotion of the new evangelization to which Pope Saint John Paul II was so urgently calling all Catholics at the time. I have been pleased to be an episcopal advisor of the apostolate from its beginning until the present.

In my conversations with Thomas, he frequently spoke about the great privilege of assisting with the visit of the International Pilgrim Virgin Statue of Our Lady of Fatima to various parts of the world and about the great favors which Our Lady obtained for the faithful on the occasion of the pilgrimages made by her statue. These favors reached even those who encountered the Statue in the context of flights to various parts of the world. Even those of seeming little faith, when they saw the Statue and the devotion of the Custodians transporting it, recognized the presence of heavenly grace.

A young adult at the time, Thomas was deeply inspired and strengthened in his Catholic faith through his mission on behalf of Our Lady of Fatima. Blessed to converse in depth with Thomas, on numerous occasions, about his devotion to Our Lady of Fatima and about his experience with the Pilgrim Virgin Statue, I am deeply grateful to him for taking the time from the demands of Catholic Action for Faith and Family to write and publish the story of his relationship with Our Eucharistic Lord under the particular care and guidance of Our Blessed Mother, Mother of Divine Grace, Our Lady of Fatima.

The International Pilgrim Virgin Statue has indeed brought countless blessings to the faithful who have been unable to make a visit to Our Lady at the holy places of her apparitions in 1917 at Fatima and yet wish to show an extraordinary sign of their love for her. Since they could not come to her, she has visited them by means of the powerful sacramental of her statue created to go on pilgrimage. Particularly inspiring is Thomas' account of the visit of the International Pilgrim Virgin Statue to Russia, the nation for which Our Lady of Fatima manifests explicitly her special maternal affection.

In a certain sense, Our Lady of Fatima has brought the holy places of her apparitions, the destination of a Fatima pilgrimage, to the faithful, so that they could come to know her better and grow in their devotion to her and, thereby, grow in the knowledge, love and service of her Divine Son. The particular grace granted through the veneration of Our Lady of Fatima, represented by the International Pilgrim Virgin Statue, is a deeper knowledge of her maternal message first communicated to Saints Francisco and Jacinta Marto and to the Servant of God Sister Lucia dos Santos. It is a message calling for prayer, especially the praying of the Holy Rosary, and penance, especially the First Saturdays of reparation for so many offenses communicated against the immeasurable and unceasing love of God represented so perfectly by the glorious pierced Heart of Jesus. Such reparation is essential to the conversion of souls and the transformation of the world.

The Message of Fatima also gives the assurance of the triumph of the Faith, of Christ, King of all hearts, through the triumph of the Immaculate Heart of Mary. As Thomas writes, the Pilgrim Virgin Statue, by God's grace, became the instrument by which the Mother of God and Mother of the Church has communicated her love to her children, as she first did to the shepherd children of Fatima from May 13 to October 13 of 1917, drawing them to her Divine Son Who alone is man's salvation. The Pilgrim Virgin Statue is certainly a woodcarving of extraordinary beauty but, through the blessing of the Church, it is endowed with an even greater beauty signifying the incomparable mystery of the Divine Maternity of the Blessed Virgin Mary, Queen of the Holy Rosary.

The beauty of the features of the Pilgrim Virgin Statue draws the devout faithful who come into its presence to contemplate and embrace the far greater beauty of their life in Christ. Faithful Christians in the presence of the Pilgrim Virgin Statue experience what the wine stewards at the Wedding Feast of Cana experienced. Approaching the Virgin Mother of God in prayer for their needs and the needs of those who have asked for their prayers, they experience a mother's love. Our Lady draws them to herself, so that she can lead them to her Divine Son, alive for us in the Church, with the counsel: "Do whatever he tells you."1 These simple words express the mystery of the Divine Maternity by which the Virgin Mary became the Mother of God, bringing God the Son Incarnate into the world and becoming His first and best disciple, and by which she continues to be the channel of all the graces which immeasurably and unceasingly pour forth from Her Divine Son's glorious pierced Heart into the hearts of His faithful sons and daughters on earthly pilgrimage to their lasting home in Heaven. To the faithful who come to her with devoted love she communicates her maternal message full of hope in the most difficult times in which the world and the Church find themselves today. The Pilgrim Virgin Statue is indeed an instrument endowed with a special blessing to convey the immense maternal love of the Blessed Virgin Mary for all mankind.

Today, the Church is beset by confusion and error about even some of her most fundamental and constant teachings. As a secular agenda continues to advance in the world, promoting the attack upon innocent and defenseless human life, upon the integrity of marriage and its incomparable fruit, the family, and upon the very freedom of man to worship God "in spirit and truth,"2 the Church herself seems confused and even at times indulgent toward a mundanity which rebels against God and His law. The world has

1 Jn 2, 5.

2 Cf. Jn 4, 23-24.

great need for the Church to announce the Faith, the truth of Christ, with clarity and courage, but sadly too often she remains silent or seems uncertain regarding the truth and its steadfast application to daily life in the world.

At Fatima, the Mother of God, our Mother, teaches us the means to go faithfully to her Divine Son and to seek from Him the wisdom and strength to bring His saving grace to a profoundly troubled world. She provides six particular means for us to employ in addressing the situation. She asks us as individual members of the faithful: 1) to pray the Rosary each day; 2) to wear the Brown Scapular; 3) to make sacrifices for the sake of saving sinners; 4) to make reparation for offenses to her Immaculate Heart by means of the First Saturday devotion; and 5) to convert our own lives ever more to Christ. Lastly, she asks the Roman Pontiff, in union with all the Bishops of the world, to consecrate Russia to her Immaculate Heart. By these means, she promises that her Immaculate Heart will triumph, bringing souls to Christ, her Son. Turning to Christ, they will make reparation for their sins. Christ, through the intercession of His Immaculate Mother, will save them from Hell and bring peace to the whole world. While the Message of Fatima is realistic about the great evils which beset the world and the Church, it is fundamentally a message of hope in the victory of the Sacred Heart of Jesus through the Immaculate Heart of Mary.

I cannot fail to comment upon Thomas' particular testimony to his profound experience of spiritual paternity connected with his devotion to the Immaculate Heart of Our Lady of Fatima. He came to know more fully and love more ardently Our Lady of Fatima through the fatherly care of Mr. John Matthias Haffert, whom he calls "Our Lady's missionary," and of Professor Plinio Corrêa de Oliveira, whom he calls "Our Lady's prophet." Both men, through their spiritual fatherhood, gave a lifelong gift to Thomas, the richness of which he has been discovering throughout the years since he first met and worked with these two extraordinary men. It is the gift which he gives to others through the apostolate, Catholic Action for Faith and the Family. Mr. Haffert and Professor Corrêa de Oliveira showed Thomas how he, as a man, was called to a deep love of the Mother of God and to the fulfillment of her requests made through her apparitions to the saintly shepherd children of Fatima.

I commend to men, in a particular way, the careful study of Chapter 4, entitled "Two Great Apostles of Our Lady," in order that they may understand how the particular gifts of manhood are needed for the spread of the Message of Fatima. Thomas' account of the devotion of these two outstanding sons of Our Lady of Fatima is also a testimonial to Divine Providence. In God's design, Mr. Haffert and Professor Corrêa de Oliveira eventually worked together to make it possible for the International Pilgrim Virgin Statue to visit many nations and to convey her message of Penitence and Peace to the whole world. The maternal direction of Our Lady of Fatima will draw souls to Christ Who will give them the sevenfold gift of the Holy Spirit for the conversion of their lives and the transformation of a culture of death into a civilization of love.

It is my hope that the reading of The Fatima Century: How the Pilgrim Virgin is Changing Our Generation will inspire many souls to unite their hearts to the Immaculate Heart of Mary in the total consecration of their hearts to the Sacred Heart of Jesus. As the Mother of God teaches us, there is no surer way to grow daily in the spiritual life and thus to become "rivers of living water"3 for a world which thirsts so much for the truth and love which are only found in the Sacred Heart of Jesus.

I desire, in a particular way, that the book will provide a significant help to the reader, helping him to center all of his labors not solely in external activity but, above all, in interior activity – participation in the Holy Sacrifice of the Mass, the Act of Thanksgiving after each Holy Mass and throughout the day, Eucharistic Adoration, the daily praying of the Holy Rosary, and the First Saturdays of reparation – by which Our Lord, through the intercession of Our Lady, transforms our lives and our world. Following Our Lord, together with His Virgin Mother, our Mother, in this way, we can be confident that the Immaculate Heart of Mary will triumph, even in our most troubled times.

May the readers of The Fatima Century: How the Pilgrim Virgin is Changing Our Generation become Eucharistic and Marian souls who are a great consolation and help to their Bishops and priests in the work of a new evangelization, in the work of teaching, celebrating and living the Catholic

---

3   Jn 7, 38.

faith with the enthusiasm and energy of the first disciples and of the first missionaries to our native places.

I praise wholeheartedly Thomas' testimony to the grace associated with the International Pilgrim Virgin Statue. May the readers experience the same grace, so that, through the maternal guidance of Our Lady of Fatima, the Immaculate Heart of the Blessed Virgin Mary will triumph over any darkness in their hearts. Through her triumph in their hearts and in the hearts of many, through the triumph of the Faith, the Immaculate Heart of Mary will also triumph over the great darkness of our time by leading souls to the truth and love of her Divine Son, by leading souls to give their hearts, with hers, completely into the Sacred Heart of Jesus.4 She will continue to speak to their hearts, as she spoke, with deepest motherly love, to the hearts of the wine stewards at Cana: "Do whatever He tells you."5

Raymond Leo Cardinal Burke
June 21, 2017

---

4   Cf. Frère Michel de la Sainte Trinité, The Whole Truth about Fatima, Volume Three: The Third Secret (1942-1960), tr. John Collorafi (Buffalo, NY: Immaculate Heart Publications, 1990), pp. 816-817.

5   Jn 2, 5.

1

HER ENCHANTING GAZE

Our Lady went into a strange country
And they crowned her for a queen,
For she needed never to be stayed or questioned
But only seen;
And they were broken down under unbearable beauty
As we have been.
~G.K. Chesterton,
"Going After the Lost Sheep"[1]

Even the most casual student of history could not be blind to the violence and upheavals of the modern world. If we were simply to limit our observations to the 20th Century, the era in which Our Lady of Fatima chose to appear, it would hardly be necessary to point out the vast drama of human suffering caused by the misuse of freedom and the tragic folly of man. It is therefore not surprising that the Virgin Mary came to our generation to help us overcome the immense sinfulness of our age. Her desire is to make us Her companions in the work of salvation through the message She gave at Fatima. There is a distinct urgency to Her message, but She will not issue thundering condemnations or attempt to scare us into cooperating with Her. She will invite us and attract us with Her sweetness and, in Chesterton's words, Her "unbearable beauty."

That is exactly the way She approached the world in 1917. In the apparitions at Fatima, Our Lady tenderly drew the three shepherd children, the direct recipients of the messages, into cooperation with Her plan of turning

---

1   G.K. Chesterton, Dennis J. Conlon, ed., *The Collected Works of G. K. Chesterton* (Collected Poetry), Vol. 10B, San Francisco: Ignatius Press, n.d.

back the tide of sin. She then appealed through them to the rest of humanity, to believers and atheists alike. And Her methods have not changed with the years: She gently draws all Her hearers into the life of grace and into the work of saving souls. All are free to accept or reject Her invitation. Our Lady doesn't need to operate in a worldly manner. She is the Mother of the King of Heaven and Earth. She uses beauty to move the world and the hearts of men.

What sets the International Pilgrim Virgin Statue apart from other religious images is Her unique and inspiring gaze. It is the singular, captivating expression of Her face that has converted souls and brought people back to Christ and to His Church. At times She looks as though She is alive. Her gaze has a distinct softening effect on people, usually in one of two ways: She can *soften a hardened situation*, such as opening a way to Christ through the ideologically-conditioned environments of Communist nations, as we will see in future chapters; or, more importantly, She can *soften hearts* to the message of conversion, which is Her real gift and Her unique contribution to the work of saving souls.

A MARIAN FORMATION

I have personally witnessed the power of Our Lady's heart-softening grace many times over the past thirty-five years, especially when I have been privileged to accompany Her on pilgrimages throughout the world. It is clear to me that when people come into contact with Her image through the Pilgrim Virgin Statue, *something happens in their souls.* My own story is perhaps a good example of this dynamic.

When I was growing up, my family was very devoted to the Blessed Virgin Mary, particularly Our Lady of Fatima and the Fatima message. We prayed the Rosary nightly and my mother and father encouraged all of their children to wear the Scapular. My early love for Our Lady was a natural part of my formative years, a presence that was absorbed through the devotional life of my family traditions and practices; but it was also the result of a deliberate project of my parents to hand on their most precious spiritual treasures to their children.

I grew up in a farming family and enjoyed many of the benefits it afforded a teenage boy. Raising and training horses, an abundance of hunting and fishing opportunities as well as the care of livestock. With this background, early in my life I was inclined to be a rancher or a veterinarian. Certainly I was religious in temperament and practice, but I was not attracted to a religious vocation as such. My ideal of life was to move to Alaska and live off the land! One day when I was speaking with my mother, she said something that had a deep effect on me: "All the hunting, fishing, and horse activities are fine," she said, "but when you go before God, what are you going to say to Him when He asks you what you did for His Kingdom?" At the time, it was hard for me to answer that question but equally hard to argue with that logic.

Our Lady of Fatima's influence, in particular, had a profound impact on my young soul. During my high school years, I remember pondering the message of Fatima and saying to myself, "If the message of Fatima is true – and I do believe it is – who am I *not* to do something about it?" I was contemplating a sort of divine imperative for my life that I couldn't ignore. I felt as though I *had to* do something about it. The truth about Fatima was a distinct divine counterbalance to my personal plans, a force of grace leading me on the narrow path to my future. I can almost say that it was a vocational call, though not in the traditional sense of a religious vocation but in the sense of an inner voice directing me to where I was to dedicate a significant portion of my life's energy.

MY PERSONAL ENCOUNTER WITH HER GAZE

In the spring of 1981 I made a trip to Latin America to visit the Brazilian Society for the Defense of Tradition, Family and Property (TFP)[2] and was privileged to meet its founder Dr. Plinio Corrêa de Oliveira. Providentially, my trip took place during the period of time that the International Pilgrim Virgin Statue was under the custody of the TFP and touring Latin America; so, while visiting Brazil I was introduced to the Pilgrim Virgin Statue for the first time at the TFP headquarters in São Paulo, and I will never forget the encounter. I can honestly say that when I laid eyes on the Statue, I fell in love with the sheer beauty of Our Lady's gaze and image in the marvelous work of

---

2   The American branch of Tradition, Family, and Property was established in the US in 1973; cf. Phillips, *Plinio*, 116.

José Thedim, the Statue's sculptor. In fact, I was struck by a sense of wonder, a highly personal experience of grace, the moment I saw the Statue. I felt as if She were looking *at* me, almost as if She had been patiently waiting for me to meet Her there. And as I would later discover, that sense of *personal encounter* is characteristic of countless souls that have come into contact with the Pilgrim Virgin Statue throughout the world.

Later that year I was given the opportunity to accompany the Statue on a week's pilgrimage through Canada. It was to be the first of my many travels with Her as one of the Custodians, and what a life-changing experience it was. Because of my temporary custodianship on that mission trip, I was able to spend a great deal of personal prayer time in the presence of Our Lady; it became apparent to me by the end of that week that I had to dedicate myself in some significant way to the promotion of the Fatima message. "Okay," I told Her. "You got me. I have to join You in this effort." And my life has never been the same.

ALL HEARTS BELONG TO HER

Our Lady can touch any heart that is open to grace. It was to Her that the Archangel Gabriel first uttered the famous truth: "For nothing shall be impossible with God" (Lk 1:37). In fact, She seems to do Her best work with the so-called impossible cases and when we least expect it. I can personally attest to Her power to transform bad situations into good through Her personal evangelization of hearts.

In 1981, when I was new in Our Lady's service, a companion Paul Folley and I were asked by the TFP to take the Statue on pilgrimage to many key Catholic historical sites in Europe. (We will speak of this pilgrimage in further detail in Chapter 9.) The Statue had been in Spain where it was undergoing a repair by three brothers who were considered the finest restorers of statuary in Europe. Paul and I went to Spain to retrieve the Statue and then to commence our European pilgrimage, which was to visit numerous sites in Spain, Germany and France. I must say, though, that I was a bit apprehensive to have such a responsibility thrust upon me. Up to that point I was a young man from California who never imagined that he would be accompanying the Pilgrim Virgin Statue on a lengthy European tour. However, when I volunteered to assist Our Lady's mission, I should have known that I'd be in for a few daunting assignments.

Like the intrepid John Haffert a generation earlier, Paul and I encountered some unexpected problems in the travel, but little did we realize at that time how handily Our Lady would work them all out. I was new to the responsibilities of custodianship, but I soon learned that I had only to be docile to Her influence and allow Her to work in the hearts of the people around me to solve every difficulty. This set a precedent that marked me for life!

A STATUE OF INESTIMABLE VALUE

On a preliminary note, many times when I'm traveling with the Statue, people will ask me what "value" the Statue has; they are seeking to know the monetary value of course. I answer that the Statue has *no value at all*, which usually surprises them. The deep significance and the miraculous aspect of this Statue in fact makes it a priceless relic of incalculable value. It is impossible to place a dollar value on it. Because of the Statue's irreplaceable character, She travels inside the airplane on a seat wherever we bring Her. To me, it always feels like I am traveling with a sacred sacramental of the Church. As Custodians, we would never allow such a treasure to be stowed in the luggage compartment.

Our custom is to buy a seat next to the Custodian and usually, when the plane has reached cruising altitude, the Custodian can open the top part of the case if anyone asks to see Her. In my experience, there have been occasions when the flight crew would find out who She was and insist that She (and I as a Custodian) be moved to the First Class cabin. It is a great tribute paid to Our Lady when lay people working in a secular environment wish to show that kind of respect to Her image. The method of transporting our precious Statue, however, is important for the story that follows.

In December of 1981, at the very end of our pilgrimage through Spain, France and Germany, we were set to return to the United States by way of the Charles De Gaulle International Airport in Paris. We arrived there for our departure, with a veritable entourage of devotees of Our Lady on hand to greet the Statue with incredible enthusiasm. While we were checking in, our hosts brought the Statue out of Her box and displayed Her on a table in the open for all passers-by to see. Much to our surprise (but it shouldn't have been) Our Lady created an "event" right there in Charles De Gaulle Airport! In the next hour or so, hundreds of people in transit through the international terminal stopped by the table to get a closer look at the Statue and to hear the stories we had to tell of the wonders that attended Her everywhere we went.

There seemed to be no barriers of language or culture at that mini-shrine to Our Lady. The Statue's beauty itself was the most eloquent witness to the message of Fatima. Most Europeans, whether religious or not, had somehow heard of the story of Fatima or were familiar with the famous event and shrine of the same name in their neighboring Portugal. As a testimony to Our Lady's divine humility, from atop a modest table in the middle of a busy airport, She was doing exactly what she was commissioned to do by the Bishop of Fatima in 1947: She was evangelizing. And what better place to do so than in the very nerve center of France, the "Eldest Daughter of the Church"? When we finally heard the call to board our flight, unbeknownst to us, the real challenge began: we had to get the Statue onto the Pan Am 747 to JFK Airport in New York.

"SHE CANNOT COME IN HERE!"

After its restoration in Spain, the Statue was packed in a padded wooden box for travel, which is what we used to transport Her through the airport to the departure gate. Her transport is different today. Even before the catastrophic events of 9/11, airport security did not easily admit people through check points and onto airplanes carrying large wooden boxes. We insisted, however, that the Statue had to find its way onto the plane because we could not run the risk of the Statue being lost with luggage, as was often the case in air travel during those years.

We got a few raised eyebrows and strange looks as we walked through the terminal with Her, but we had remarkably little trouble getting the box through the security lines that day. When we went to board the plane, how-ever, the padded box presented an immediate problem: it was just too big.

Although it fit through the cabin door, it was physically larger than airline regulations allowed – a four-foot by three-foot rectangular box was hardly carry-on luggage. And it didn't fit very well in an airline seat. One of the crew members came and rather angrily demanded to know, "Where is this box going?" I responded somewhat naively, "Well it's a Statue and no one said we couldn't bring it in here." To which she shot back, "No, this box cannot come in here. This is against FAA regulations."

Word was quickly spreading among the flight attendants about the unwieldy box taking up three seats in cabin class, and the crew at this point was decidedly unhappy. They called an officious man, the flight engineer or navigator, who apparently was responsible for storage on the plane, and when he saw the box he also said, "Look, this is absolutely impossible. This box can't stay here, it has to leave." But since we were virtually the last people to board the plane – and the only ones bearing a huge box – the crew members were in a hurry to resolve the issue. The flight engineer reiterated with some force, "This box has to go out, it has to go underneath with the luggage." At that, we said, "If it's going underneath with the luggage, then the Statue is coming out," whereupon we took the Statue out of the box and placed Her in a seat between us which, fortunately, was free just then despite the jumble of passengers settling in. Then we snapped the seat belt around the Statue and sat down on either side of Her to get ready for take-off.

The crew brusquely picked up the padded box to remove it to the baggage compartment, but the cabin door was already closed. This added further emotional tension to our dilemma: the crew had a bulky and unwanted box on the plane, and they were not very happy with the two young men who brought it on. They also made their irritation very clear through a rather frigid aloofness toward us. The crew secured the box in three economy seats as the plane went airborne. The friction of the encounter weighed on us as the plane took off and the perspiration on our brows dissipated.

This situation turned out to be what is commonly called a baptism by fire – it was the first trip for both Paul and I as Custodians. Understandably, we were exhausted by the attitude and tone of the crew, but it was also evident that the crew felt the same way toward us. Only later did I reach the point in my reflections where I could sympathize with the flight crew's frustration. Paul and I had violated airline rules, albeit unwittingly, by bringing the box on the plane. I could only imagine how many times the crew on that international flight had to deal with other people wanting to bend or break rules to transport something of value for their own reasons. Then again, my empathy for the flight crew was limited: *no one* had the priceless treasure we had.

As the plane took off, we looked at each other past the Statue seated between us and did the best thing we knew how to do in a stressful situation: we prayed. "Let's say three Hail Mary's," we agreed, "because we're with Our Lady. We'll put this in Her hands. There's nothing we can do here."

The stress caused by our grand entry into the jetliner was not the only matter weighing on us. We were also anticipating the next day's arrival at JFK International Airport in New York where a large entourage would be waiting to greet and officially welcome the Statue back to the United States. At that moment, however, we were a mission team with challenges: the box was up front, the Statue was separated from it and the rest of our luggage, the flight crew was annoyed at us, and Our Lady's two neophyte Custodians were both exhausted and concerned. We had so many things to put in order in such a short time, ourselves included. We had gotten on the plane, but we had no idea how things were going to work out when we would arrive at JFK.

Inspired by our faith we quietly recited our three Hail Mary's and just sat there in silence for a while, preoccupied about what was going to happen and feeling very much alone. The prayer gave us peace however. As we put all matters in Our Lady's hands little did we know how much our trust in Her would be rewarded. She always arranges situations and resolves problems in such a way that things always turn out better than if we had never had the difficulties in the first place. That dramatic turn-around effect, that ability to bring good out of every possible difficulty is the hallmark of sanctity, indeed, infallible evidence of the presence of the pre-eminent Saint of our spiritual family. And Our Lady did not disappoint.

AN ASTONISHING VISIT FROM THE CEO

Once the plane reached cruising altitude, a middle-aged woman unexpectedly came up to us and introduced herself. She said she was an American and that she was with a group that was returning from Ireland after a two week journey. They had seen the Statue on display in the airport and were simply *overwhelmed* to know that the famous International Pilgrim Virgin State was on that same flight. Her quiet enthusiasm was palpable, and I might add, contagious. Her interest immediately brought us out of our doldrums. She said that many in her group were actually moved to tears that they were traveling on the same plane as the Pilgrim Virgin Statue and that they could not help but see a marvelous act of Providence that the flight was on the very feast day of the Immaculate Conception, December 8th. Our visitor went on to tell us that if there was anything we needed, we should not hesitate to ask. It was an attractive offer, as *their* group was seated in First Class.

A few minutes later, a well-dressed middle-aged man approached and said, "Gentlemen, I was just told by my friend here, Mrs. So-and-So, that this is the famous Pilgrim Virgin Statue of Our Lady of Fatima. I'm part of the group that is coming back from Ireland, and I cannot get over this. I wanted to express to you how graced and privileged we are to have Her here."[3] He asked us a few questions about the Statue and our recent mission, and we took the opportunity to witness to him about the mysteries of the Fatima event. Soon, he took out a business card and handed it to me and said, "If there is anything that I can do to help – let me know." I somewhat perfunctorily accepted the card and tucked it away in my coat pocket without looking at it as I thanked him for his good wishes.

The gentleman then asked, "Does the Captain and the crew know what they have on board here?" Paul and I looked at each other with a nervous glance, and I responded sheepishly, "Well, they know the Statue's on board." We were a little embarrassed to fill him in on the details of our grand entrance onto the plane.. We cringed to think what he would "find out" if he spoke with the flight crew.

Two or three minutes later, to our great amazement, the Captain of the 747 came over the loudspeaker and addressed the passengers with the following message: *"This is your Captain speaking. I have just been informed that we have the privilege to be transporting tonight on our flight the famous International Pilgrim Statue of Our Lady of Fatima."* After Paul and I picked our jaws up from the floor, we looked at each other with huge smiles on our faces, astonished

---

3   The dialogue in this story comes from my 2003 interview with *Crusade* Magazine, slightly edited for clarity.

to hear the *Captain* of this mammoth jetliner announcing the presence of the Pilgrim Virgin to all on board. He explained to the passengers that the Statue had just been restored and was currently returning to the United States after having been on pilgrimage in Europe. He added a few more details as well.

It occurred to me at that moment that the man who had given us his business card must have had a certain amount of clout with the airline to be able to inspire the Captain to make such an announcement on short notice. When I reached in my pocket to pull out his business card, the mystery of who we had been talking to was made manifest: he was the *Chief Executive Officer* of Pan Am itself! I was overwhelmed contemplating the odds that the head of the principal and largest international air carrier in the United States, one considered a cultural icon of the 20th Century and the unofficial overseas flag carrier, just happened to be on this flight with the Pilgrim Virgin.

One grace built upon another and soon the crew members who previously had been so upset at us came to our seats wanting to see the Statue up close and offering their help if we should need anything. The frosty flight engineer too came up with a warm smile and offered his assistance, and this time we took him up on it. We told him that we would probably need help getting the Statue off the plane with all of our luggage and other materials, and he listened to our concern with great attention. He promised that as soon as we were in range of JFK, he would radio ahead and arrange everything for us. He told us that we had absolutely nothing to worry about.

Thereafter, the entire tenor of our flight experience changed. The crew could not have been more helpful – in fact, they seemed to be more interested in getting pictures of the Statue than anyone else on the flight. Even the Captain and the Co-Pilot came cabin-side to see the Statue and visit with us. What an amazing turn-around, all in the space of about an hour. This was all brought about by three Hail Mary's.

ALL OBSTACLES REMOVED

As the plane prepared for landing at JFK the flight engineer came to us again and informed us that he had arranged for someone to come on board and help us with our belongings (including the padded box) so that we, the Custodians, could carry Our Lady's Statue in procession into the terminal where the waiting entourage was greatly anticipating Her arrival. We told him how extremely grateful we were for his help and marveled at how Our Lady had orchestrated this whole matter to reach such a positive conclusion. But every victory is usually preceded by a set-back, and we encountered ours immediately as we exited the plane. The man who was designated to help us did in fact help but only to a point. He got us to the waiting area, deposited our luggage and materials, and then, surprisingly, said he had to go. His departure effectively left us stranded in the customs area unable to manage the trek through the labyrinth of customs and immigration procedures.

Once again, the two Custodians found ourselves in a bind, completely unable to lug all our belongings through customs. We placed the Statue on a table and stood overlooking the Immigration area where our helper had deposited us, and contemplated our next move. We wanted Our Lady to arrive in procession and not in a padded box but we were not in much of a position to provide Her that dignified entrance into the terminal. Even in 1981 getting through JFK customs from an international flight was a complicated process. We were feeling overwhelmed again, but just at that moment the same lady who had first approached us in the plane came up to us again and asked if we needed help. When we explained our dilemma she promptly said, "Give me your passports," and then ordered us: "Wait here, I'll be right back," as she hurried away.

Five minutes later she returned with the *Director of the entire Immigration section of the airport.* How our friend made contact with him I will never know. The man admitted that he hardly ever came down to the floor from his office above the waiting area but he did so that day. Even better, he was beside himself with joy at the presence of the Statue. He pulled a Scapular out of his shirt and held it up as if it were a trophy, saying with genuine enthusiasm, "I was just *baptized* this week, and I just received First Communion and this Scapular. And I can't believe that I am here now, here in the presence of the Statue." A better outcome we could not have expected. He asked if he could kiss the Statue, and I immediately invited him to kiss Her feet, which he promptly did with an expression of profound devotion.

We spent a minute or two talking with the Director and then, as if awoken, he realized that he had to get us out to the waiting crowd. "Hold on," he said as he ran off with our passports. When he returned a few minutes later he said, "Your passports are stamped – follow me." He made sure that one of his workers collected all of our luggage and materials as well as the padded box, and he personally escorted us out – through customs, through immigration, through every check point – to the place where hundreds of people received Our Blessed Mother with thunderous applause. As Paul and I emerged into the terminal amid such acclamation, I felt a profound sense of gratitude and consolation. More importantly, it was a deeply moving experience for us to see that Our Lady received the honor She deserved and that so many individuals who work in secular jobs had put their duties aside and put their religion first, without compromising anyone's safety or security. All the obstacles we feared had somehow miraculously vanished. All the problems we imagined would only get worse were somehow, incredibly and happily, resolved. Only a heavenly Lady could accomplish that for us.

THE INSPIRING STORY
OF THE FATIMA APPARITIONS

Fatima is one of the greatest signs of the times in the 20th century
because it announces many of the later events, and conditions them
on the response to its appeals.
~Pope John Paul II, October 13th, 1991[4]

In order to talk more at length about the International Pilgrim Virgin Statue, it is first necessary to present an overview of the Fatima apparitions and the circumstances in which Our Lady brought this message to the world. The story has an inspirational appeal like no other.

THE SETTING

Founded in 1568, the municipality of Vila Nova de Ourem, roughly ninety miles from Lisbon, sits perched among the low hills of the Aire mountain range in the center of Portugal. One of its villages is called Fatima, a name that is of Islamic origin: Fatima was the daughter of Mohammed. The entire district in which the municipality is located is a barren landscape of rocky soil and limestone. In 1917, the year of the Marian apparitions to the three shepherd children, another village in the municipality was called Aljustrel, about one mile from Fatima. The three children to whom Our Lady appeared were born and lived in Aljustrel. The protagonists of the beautiful story of Fatima were Lucia dos Santos (age 10 at the time of the apparitions), and

---

4   Published in the *L'Osservatore Romano*, 10/24/91.

Lucia's cousins, Francisco and Jacinta Marto (ages 9 and 7 respectively).[5] Francisco and Jacinta's mother was the sister of Lucia's father.

Two miles west of Fatima lies the Cova da Iria, a broad, sloping meadow that resembled a natural amphitheater. The land was owned by Lucia's father and was the place where the three children would bring their families' flocks of sheep for grazing. It became the place where Our Lady appeared five times to the children from May to October of that year.

THE THREE APPARITIONS OF THE ANGEL OF PORTUGAL

In the spring of 1916 the three children were playing in front of a cave located on a hill near Fatima when a bright angel appeared to them with a message. This angel identified himself as the *Angel of Peace* and later as the *Angel of Portugal*. The apparition took place in this manner: the three children felt a strong wind that shook the trees and noticed some distance away, "a light whiter than snow, and transparent, gleaming most brilliantly, like a crystal of great beauty through which the sun's rays glisten."[6] The light drew near to them, and in the light, they could make out the form of an extremely handsome young man that Lucia judged to be about fifteen years of age. They were astonished by the apparition, and immediately absorbed in it, when suddenly the Angel spoke to them.

"*Do not fear,*" he said. "*I am the Angel of Peace. Pray with me.*" The Angel himself knelt down on the terrain in front of the cave and bowed his head to the ground. The three children imitated him and repeated his words: "*My God, I believe, I adore, I hope and I love You. I implore Your pardon for those who do not believe, do not adore, do not hope and do not love You.*"

The Angel prayed this prayer three times and rising, said, "*Pray that way. The Hearts of Jesus and Mary are attentive to the voice of your supplications.*" Thereupon the Angel disappeared and the three children said nothing about this apparition to anyone afterwards. In fact, they were so deeply

---

5   The children were born on March 22, 1907 (Lucia), June 11, 1908 (Francisco), and March 11, 1910 (Jacinta).

6   Joseph A. Pelletier, *The Sun Danced at Fatima* (New York: Image Doubleday, 1983), 18. The story of the apparitions comes from the series of *Memoirs* that Lucia wrote in stages during the years 1935 to 1941 when she was a nun with the Dorothean Sisters. Except where otherwise noted, the translation of the dialogue from Sr. Lucia's *Memoirs* is taken from Fr. Pelletier's work, cited above, Chapters 1-18.

affected by the experience that they were hardly able to speak at all for the next day. It was a profound experience of heavenly grace, and it left their souls in a state of awe-filled silence.

Several months later, in the summer of 1916, the Angel of Portugal made a second visit to the children, this time at the bottom of a sloping field near Jacinta and Francisco's home. The children were playing by a well in the field, and the Angel immediately called out to them, *"What are you doing? Pray, pray a great deal. The Hearts of Jesus and Mary have designs of mercy on you. Offer prayers and sacrifices continuously to the Most High."*

Lucia asked him, "How are we to offer sacrifices?" and the Angel responded: *"Make a sacrifice of everything that you can, and offer it to the Lord as an act of reparation for the sins by which He is offended and of supplication for the conversion of sinners. In this way you will draw peace upon our country. I am its guardian angel, the Angel of Portugal. Above all, accept and bear with submission the suffering that the Lord will send you."* Following this apparition too, the children again experienced such a sense of awe and wonder that they could barely speak for the next several hours.

The third apparition of the Angel took place at the end beginning of the fall of 1916. Sister Lucia later described the apparition in these words:

While we were there the Angel appeared to us for the third time. He held a chalice in his hands with a Host above it. Some drops of blood were falling from the Host into the sacred vessel. Leaving the chalice and the hose suspended in the air, the Angel prostrated himself on the ground and repeated this prayer three times:

Most Holy Trinity, Father, Son, Holy Spirit, I adore You profoundly and I offer You the most precious Body, Blood, Soul and Divinity of Jesus Christ, present in all the tabernacles of the world, in reparation for the outrages, sacrileges and indifference by which He Himself is offended. By the infinite merits of His Most Sacred Heart and the Immaculate Heart of Mary, I beg of You the conversion of poor sinners.

Then, rising, he once more took the Chalice and the Host in his hands. He gave the Host to me, and to Jacinta and Francisco he gave the contents of the Chalice to drink, saying as he did so:

Take and drink the Body and the Blood of Jesus Christ, horribly outraged by the sins of ungrateful men. Make reparation for their crimes and console your God.'

Once again he prostrated himself on the ground and repeated the same prayer with us three more times, *'Most Holy Trinity . . . etc.'* and disappeared.[7]

It is widely recognized that the Angel's role was to prepare the souls of the children to meet Our Lady and to condition their minds to embrace several of the key elements of the message that She would give them: prayer, reparation, sacrifice for sinners, Eucharistic devotion. Although Lucia had received her First Holy Communion the year before, the Angel of Portugal was the effective minister of this most Blessed Sacrament to the two littler children. It is hard to fathom, but Francisco, who died two years later, had not received Holy Communion from the hand of a priest until his Viaticum.[8]

THE FIRST APPARITION OF OUR LADY

The first apparition of Our Lady took place on May 13th, 1917 at the Cova da Iria where the children were pasturing their flocks. Our Lady appeared above a small tree, which stood about three foot high, called a holm oak. Similar to the Angel's first apparition, the Lady from heaven used a heavenly sign to alert the children to Her presence. In this case the sign was a series of flashes in the sky that they said resembled lightning. The children thought a storm was coming and began to gather the sheep when suddenly a radiantly beautiful lady was standing before them atop the small tree. Lucia described this lady as a woman "dressed all in white. She was more brilliant than the sun and radiated a light more clear and intense than a crystal glass filled with sparkling water when the rays of the burning sun shine through it."[9] As if to show that Our Lady treats each person with a completely unique kind

7   John M. Haffert, *Her Own Words to the Nuclear Age: The Memoirs of Sr. Lucia* (Asbury: The 101 Foundation, Inc., 1993), 247.

8   Fr. Andrew Apostoli, CFR, *Fatima for Today* (San Francisco: Ignatius Press, 2010), 138. For those not familiar with the expression, Viaticum is the Latin term for the final reception of Holy Communion before a person departs from this life. It means, literally, "with you on the way".

9   Haffert, *Her Own Words*, 248.

of love, each of the children had a slightly different experience of Our Lady: Lucia could see, hear, and speak to Her. Jacinta both saw and heard Her but could not speak to Her while Francisco neither heard nor spoke to Her but could see Her appearances.

Sensing their initial fear, Our Lady said, "Do not be afraid. I will not harm you."

"Where are You from?" asked Lucia.

"I am from heaven," the Lady responded.

"What is it that You want of me?" said Lucia.

"I have come to ask the three of you to come here for six consecutive months, on the thirteenth day, at this same hour. Then I will tell you who I am and what I want. Afterward I will return here again a seventh time."

In her childhood simplicity Lucia then asked, "Will I go to Heaven?"

"Yes, you will," said the Lady.

"And Jacinta?"

"Yes."

"And Francisco?"

"He too will go, but he must say many beads." (That is, Rosaries.)

Then, Lucia inquired about two girls from the village who had recently died. "Is Maria das Neves in heaven?"

"Yes."

"And Amelia?"

"She will be in purgatory until the end of the world." This seemingly harsh fate was not greeted with bewilderment by little Lucia who many years later as an adult commented about this statement: "Is it so unbelievable that a soul could be in Purgatory until the end of time," said the nun, "when for one mortal sin a soul can be in Hell for all eternity?" Sr. Lucia made this astonishing comment to Mr. Haffert during their four hour interview in 1946, when she had the maturity and education to understand the theological significance of Our Lady's words.[10]

Our Lady then asked the children: "Are you willing to offer yourselves to God and bear all the suffering He wishes to send you, as an act of reparation

---

10. *Soul* Magazine, "Hope for the World," 1952; see also, Russia *Will Be Converted* (Washington, New Jersey: AMI International Press, 1954) and *Sign of Her Heart* (Washington, New Jersey: Ave Maria Institute, 1971).

for the sins by which He is offended and of supplication for the conversion of sinners?"

Their response was an enthusiastic, "Yes, we are willing!"

"Then you will have much to suffer," said Our Lady, "but the grace of God will be your comfort." As Our Lady said these words, Lucia recounts that She opened her hands for the first time, communicating to us a light so intense that, as it streamed from Her hands, its rays penetrated our hearts and the innermost depths of our souls, making us see ourselves in God, who was this light, more clearly than we see ourselves in the best of mirrors. Then, moved by an intimate impulse that was also communicated to us, we fell on our knees repeating in our hearts, *'O Most Holy Trinity, I adore You! My God, my God, I love You in the most Blessed Sacrament!'*

And Our Lady added, "Say the beads each day, to attain peace for the world and the end of the War." She then rose toward the skies and disappeared.

We should note, in passing, that the children experienced the apparition of Our Lady quite differently than they did the apparition of the Angel of Portugal. During and after Our Lady's visit the children felt a profound sense of peace, joy, and even happiness at Her presence. They did not feel tongue-tied or stunned as they did after the appearance of the Angel. In fact, they were overwhelmed with joy and ready to do all that Our Lady asked: to pray, to witness to their experiences, and above all, to offer themselves to God as a pleasing sacrifice for the world.

On this matter, the holy Angel had asked the children to pray in reparation for the "outrages and sacrileges" by which Our Blessed Lord is offended; Our Lady asked for the conversion of the offenders. Little did the children know how prophetic those requests were! It is a little known fact that the first act of the Communist revolution in Russia took place in the capital city of Moscow *on the precise day* of Our Lady's appearance in Portugal, May 13th, 1917. On that day a band of murderous troops exploded into one of the Catholic churches in Moscow and galloped up the main aisle on horseback. They bounded into the sanctuary and destroyed the altar; they proceeded to smash holy images and statues in the side altars and then invaded the catechism classes that were taking place at that very moment.[11] In their diabolical wrath, they killed a number of children who were learning about the Catholic Faith. The desecration of holy places and the murder of innocents would be twin pillars of the Communist revolution for the next century.

THE SECOND APPARITION

Faithful to Our Lady's wishes, the children went to the Cova da Iria at noon on the 13th day of the next month, June, 1917. The seers were accompanied by about fifty people. In the interim, little Jacinta had promised Lucia that she would keep the first apparition a secret but had been unable to do so. She told her mother about the beautiful Lady that had appeared to them. News of this sort spread quickly in the little village. When Our Lady appeared once again in a flash of light, Lucia called everyone's attention to Her arrival and began the dialogue: "What do you want of me?"

"I want you to come here on the thirteenth of the coming month, and I want you to recite the beads every day. I desire that you learn to read. Later I will tell you what I want," said the heavenly Visitor.

Lucia remembers that she had promised someone to ask Our Lady for the cure of a sick person, and Our Lady responded, "Tell him that if he converts himself he will be cured within a year."

Lucia then boldly asked, "I would like to ask you to take us to heaven."

"Yes," responded Our Lady, "I will take Jacinta and Francisco within a short while, but you are to remain here on earth for some time longer. Jesus wants to use you to make me known and loved. He wants to establish in the world the devotion to my Immaculate Heart. To those who embrace it, I promise salvation. These souls will be loved by God as flowers placed by me to adorn His throne."

"Am I to remain here alone?" Lucia asked despondently.

"No, my daughter," the heavenly Mother replied. "Does this cause you to suffer much? Don't be discouraged. I will never abandon you. My Immaculate Heart will be your refuge and the way that will lead you to God."

11   Rt. Rev. Msgr. Fulton J. Sheen, D.D., *The Scapular* Magazine, "Russia and Our Lady," March-April, 1951.

Then, just as She had done the previous month, Our Lady opened her arms (as the priest does at Mass when he invites people to pray) and communicated to the children another ray of an intense light that penetrated their hearts with Christ's love. Before Our Lady's open right hand was a Heart surrounded and pierced by thorns. The children understood it to be the Immaculate Heart of Mary, outraged by the sins of humanity and seeking reparation. Then Our Lady was once again lifted up toward the sun in the east and disappeared.

THE THIRD APPARITION

The following month, July 13th, 1917, Our Lady again appeared, and this time there were between two and three thousand people present. She arrived in the same way as in the previous two months and Lucia began the conversation in a similar fashion: "What do you want of me today?"

Our Lady repeated a previous request, adding a new element: "I want you to come here on the thirteenth of the coming month and to continue to say the beads every day in honor of Our Lady of the Rosary to obtain peace for the world and the end of the war, for she alone can succor you."

Lucia spoke frankly again: "I would like to ask you to tell us who you are. And would you perform a miracle so that everyone will believe that you are appearing to us?"

To this, Our Lady responds, "Continue to come here every month. In October I will tell you who I am and what I want. And I shall perform a miracle that all will see, in order that they may believe." Our Lady then added, "Sacrifice yourselves for sinners and repeat often, especially whenever you make a sacrifice for them: '*O Jesus, it is for love of Thee, for the conversion of sinners and in reparation for the sins committed against the Immaculate Heart of Mary.*'"

Then, parting Her hands as before, the beams of light now shot downward and penetrated the earth instead of their hearts, and a vast chasm was opened up before their eyes. At that moment, the horrified children were given a vision of the pains and fires of Hell. Here is how Sr. Lucia described the frightening experience in her *Memoirs*:

The rays of light penetrated the earth, and we saw as it were a sea of fire. Plunged in this fire were demons and souls in human form, like transparent burning embers, all blackened or burnished bronze, floating about in the conflagration, now raised into the air by the flames that issued from within themselves together with great clouds of smoke, now falling back on every side like sparks in huge fires without weight or equilibrium amid shrieks and groans of pain and despair, which horrified us and made us tremble with fear. (It must have been this sight which caused me to cry out, as people say they heard me.) The demons could be distinguished by their terrifying and repellent likeness to frightful and unknown animals, black and transparent like burning coals.[12]

The terrible vision of hell lasted but a moment, and Lucia later admitted that they might have died of fright had the vision lasted any longer. Our Lady again spoke to the children after the vision:

You have seen hell, where the souls of poor sinners go. To save them God wants to establish in the world the devotion to my Immaculate Heart. If people do what I shall tell you, many souls will be saved and there will be peace. The war is going to end, but if people do not stop offending God, another and worse one will begin in the reign of Pius XI. When you see a night illuminated by an unknown light, know that it is the great sign that God is giving you that He is going to punish the world for its crimes by means of war, famine, and persecution of the Church and of the Holy Father.

To prevent this, I shall come to ask for the consecration of Russia to my Immaculate Heart and for Communions of Reparation on the First Saturdays. If they heed my requests, Russia will be converted and there will be peace. If not, she will spread her errors throughout the world, promoting wars and persecution of the Church, the good will be martyred, the Holy Father will have much to suffer, various nations will be annihilated.

In the end, my Immaculate Heart will triumph. The Holy Father will consecrate Russia to me, and she will be converted, and a certain period of peace will be granted to the world. In Portugal the dogma of

12   Haffert, Her Own Words, 254.

Faith will be always preserved. Do not tell this to anyone.[13] But you may tell Francisco about it.

Our Lady continued with instructions for the children: "When you recite the beads, say after each mystery: *'O my Jesus, forgive us, save us from the fire of hell; lead all souls to heaven, especially those in greatest need [in greatest danger of damnation]'.*"

"Isn't there anything else that you want of me?" asked Lucia, as if the vision of Hell were not enough for one day!

"No," Our Lady replied, "today I want nothing further from you," and She began to rise toward the east until She disappeared.

THE FOURTH APPARITION

With the growing popularity of the apparitions and the prediction of three more to come, the atheistic administrator (i.e., governor) of the region abducted the three children and put them in prison overnight, causing them to miss the apparition of August 13th believing that this would stifle interest. Nonetheless, Our Lady appeared at the site of the Cova that day in a form that was visible and audible to the people who showed up expecting the apparition. Most of the people there reported hearing a loud thunder clap at the noon hour and saw a light cloud hovering over the holm oak. Some acknowledged that the sun dimmed when the cloud came, and others saw the crowd bathed in kaleidoscopic colors and hues. What they did not see, however, were the children. They had been kidnapped by the administrator and subject to his truly immoral interrogations and threats through which he tried to get them to renounce their witness to Our Lady and to reveal the secrets She had entrusted to them. The children remained steadfast in their fidelity to Our Lady and preferred to die rather than betray Her trust. After spending time amidst criminals in the local jail, they were released by the administrator on August 15th, the feast of Our Lady's Assumption.

---

13   On May 13th, 2000 the Holy See disclosed the third part of the secret. The disclosure gave rise to heated debates about its contents. To deal with these issues here would require a great deal of space and would deviate from the main focus of this book, which is the Pilgrim Virgin Statue.

According to Sr. Lucia, Our Lady appeared to them on the very day of their release while others remember that it was on the following Sunday after their release, that is, August 19th. Whatever the actual date, while the children were tending their flocks at Os Valinhos, a property near their home, Our Lady appeared to the three children once again with the familiar flash of light. Lucia began the conversation in the familiar way: "What do you want of me?"

"I want you to continue going to the Cova da Iria on the thirteenth of the month," replied Our Lady, "and to keep on reciting the beads every day. In the last month I will perform a miracle so that all may believe."[14] Our Lady then added, "Pray, pray very much, and make sacrifices for sinners, for many souls go to hell because they have no one to make sacrifice and to pray for them." The vision finished with these words, and Our Lady once again rose toward the east and disappeared.

THE FIFTH APPARITION

The atheist administrator's kidnapping and interrogation of the children in August had the exact opposite effect of what he had intended. In the face of imprisonment and even the threat of death, the children's candor, consis tency, and refusal to violate their word to Our Lady only increased public interest in the apparitions. For that reason, on September 13th, approximately thirty thousand people showed up at the Cova da Iria to be present at the promised apparition. This time Our Lady came in a sort of luminous globe gliding gracefully from east to west, a sign that everyone present could see. When the globe settled again on the little oak tree, it was immediately sur rounded by a dense cloud and something like white flower petals fell from the sky that a good number of the people present could see with their own eyes. Lucia began again in her typical fashion: "What do you want of me?"

"Continue to say the beads so as to bring about the end of the war," said Our Lady. "In October Our Lord will come, and so will Our Lady of Sorrows and Our Lady of Mount Carmel. Saint Joseph will also come with the Child

---

14   For the sake of brevity we have skipped over a few homely details of the apparitions such as prayer requests.

Jesus to bless the world." Then Our Lady added a personal recommendation to the children about their penances: "God is pleased with your sacrifice, but He does not want you to sleep with the rope. Wear it only during the day." Our Lady was referring to a common ascetical practice of the time of tying a rope around some part of the body to cause discomfort as a sacrifice to God. Finally, Lucia spoke to Our Lady about a personal problem. "There are many who say that I am an impostor and that I deserve to be hanged and burned. Please perform a miracle so that all will believe!" To this request Our Lady simply reiterated Her earlier promise: "Yes, in October I will perform a miracle so that all may believe."

When Our Lady departed, many present saw the globe rise from the tree and return the way it had come until it had disappeared into the east.

THE SIXTH APPARITION

The time of the promised public miracle had arrived, October 13th, 1917. Estimates of between seventy and one hundred thousand people had traveled to the Cova da Iria amidst a dreary downpour of rain. The immense crowd was praying the Rosary when Our Lady appeared upon the holm oak. Lucia seemed to be lost in wonder as she beheld Our Lady's beauty, so little Jacinta nudged her and said, "Lucia, talk to Our Lady! She is already there waiting." Lucia, the official spokesperson for the group, began as usual: "What do you want of me?"

"I want a chapel built here in honor of the Lady of the Rosary. Continue without fail to say the beads every day. The war is going to end and the soldiers will soon return to their homes."

"Will you tell me what your name is?" asked Lucia, who had been waiting for six months for this information.

"I am the Lady of the Rosary," replied the beautiful Lady.

Lucia added, "I have many favors to ask. Many people seek cures and conversions."

"I will grant some requests but not all of them. They must amend their lives and ask forgiveness for their sins," Our Lady replied. With sadness, She added, "People must not offend Our Lord anymore, for He is already greatly offended." These were the final words of the heavenly Lady to the children, and as She rose and disappeared into the sky, Lucia cried out, "Look at the sun!"

While the people were gazing at the sun, which they could see without the slightest damage to their eyes, the three children saw something in the sky that the rest of the crowd could not see. They beheld Saint Joseph with the Child Jesus standing next to the sun together with Our Lady who was dressed in a white tunic with a blue mantle. Both Saint Joseph and the Child Jesus were dressed in red and appeared to bless the world. This vision changed and Lucia alone saw Our Lord as an adult dressed in red and blessing the crowd with Our Lady of Sorrows dressed in purple near Him. This vision was followed by another change of light, and Lucia then saw Our Lady appearing as Our Lady of Mount Carmel and holding the scapular in Her right hand, in fulfillment of Her promise to appear in this form. Lucia was later to comment that Our Lady appeared holding the scapular because she wants everyone to wear it.

THE MIRACLE OF THE SUN

As these scenes continued, the crowd witnessed the miracle promised by Our Lady. It had been pouring down rain the entire day; all of a sudden the clouds parted, the rain ceased, and the sun shone through them like a large silver disk. It shone brightly, but the people could look directly at it without harm to their eyes. The disk began to spin and then it suddenly stopped. It quickly started again and became like a huge ball of fire. It threw off flames of fire into the sky in a frightening whirlwind as it continued to rotate. Three times the sun appeared to zigzag in the sky above the terrorized crowd. The phenomenon reached its peak intensity when it appeared to plunge headlong from the sky downward to the earth, causing many in the crowd to cry out that the world was coming to the end and to beg for mercy. In an instant, the sun zigzagged back to its usual position in the sky and began to shine like normal.

When the stunned crowd looked at their rain-soaked clothes, they found that they were completely dry, as was the entire area that had been a mass of mud just moments before. The solar phenomenon lasted for about ten minutes and was witnessed by people as far away as thirty miles from

Fatima, thus discrediting the claims that this was just a case of mass hysteria. In fact, the miracle was witnessed and accurately reported on by atheists as well as people of faith, and it decisively confirmed all that Our Lady had said during the past six months. John Haffert was to note, quite perceptively, "As far as we know, this is *the only occasion in history when the exact time and place of a public miracle was predicted "so that everyone [would] believe"* (emphasis in original).[15]

OUR LADY TAKES JACINTA AND FRANCISCO TO HERSELF

In the second apparition, Our Lady had forewarned that both Francisco and Jacinta would not be long for this world. Soon after the apparitions were completed, Francisco and Jacinta both died, victims of the worldwide influenza epidemic that swept the globe after the First World War. Francisco passed away on April 4th, 1919, and Jacinta died within a year of her brother, on February 20th, 1920, after telling Our Lady that she wished to suffer longer for souls. And suffer she did. After enduring incompetent medical care, a number of useless surgeries (without anesthesia), and the effects of pleurisy, Our Lady took Jacinta to Herself on the exact day and hour that She had predicted.

In the same apparition, Our Lady told Lucia that she would remain after her cousins had gone to heaven and that God would use the remaining seer to spread devotion to Her Immaculate Heart. This prediction was fulfilled in a remarkable way. Lucia lived to one month short of her ninety-eighth birthday and died on February 13th, 2005, a faithful witness to the message of Fatima for nearly nine decades.

---

15   John M. Haffert, *The World's Greatest Secret* (Washington, New Jersey: Ave Maria Institute, 1967), 170.

3

A STATUE FOR THE WORLD

One day Our Lady will be carried around the world in triumph.[16]
~St. Catherine Labouré, 1806-1876.

A necessary duty before we begin our narrative is to document the existence of various Fatima statues so that we can clearly distinguish the Statue whose story we are telling in this book. We must also clarify the process by which the International Pilgrim Virgin Statue came into existence.

It is necessary to mention in passing that Catholics have always venerated holy statues, paintings, icons, and other forms of sacred art to recall the person or thing depicted. Just as it helps to remember one's mother by looking at her photograph so it helps to recall the example of the saints by looking at images of them. Catholics never adore statues but solemnly venerate them as a means of increasing devotion and fervor of faith. This is important to keep in mind as we look at the fascinating history of the many Fatima statues, a history which begins with the original image created in 1920 to commemorate the supernatural apparitions of the Mother of God to three young children that had taken place just three years earlier.

THE ORIGINAL STATUE

On the third anniversary of the apparitions, May 13th, 1920, during the period

16   Louis Kaczmarek, *The Wonders She Performs* (Manassas: Trinity Communications, 1986), 36; John M. Haffert, *Dear Bishop! Memoirs of the Author Concerning the History of the Blue Army* (Washington, New Jersey: AMI International Press, 1982), 290.

of the anti-Catholic, atheistic government, a wealthy Portuguese man named Gilberto Fernandes dos Santos, a resident of Torres Novas, went to Fatima intending to disrupt the prayerful celebration of the pilgrims who came for the anniversary. It is said that he arrived there as a persecutor but went home as a defender and promoter of the Fatima event.

Apparently, the overall environment of peace and prayer surrounding the event deeply affected Senhor Fernandes. As he watched the people he had intended to harass, he was impressed with the personal conversions and pious demeanor of the people as well as the evident holiness of the site of the apparitions and its environs. Our Lady, as She so often does, must have touched Fernandes' heart on that day because, contrary to the original intention that drove him there, his conversion at the place of apparitions of Our Lady of Fatima was to have an enormous impact for good.

In gratitude for the spiritual serenity that he drew from the graces obtained in Fatima, Fernandes commissioned José Ferreira Thedim – called "the Michelangelo of Portugal"[17] – to create a statue of the Virgin Mary who had appeared at the Cova da Iria. Little did the sculptor know at the time that this statue was to be just the first of four statues of Our Lady of Fatima that he would sculpt in the next thirty years and that would be crucial in spreading the Fatima message throughout the world. With this and the subsequent statues, Thedim apparently had the help of his younger brother, Guilherme, who was a gifted sculptor/artist in his own right.

When the statue was brought for its solemn consecration and enshrinement at the site of the apparitions, the crowds were greeted by armed Portuguese soldiers of the Communist government who tried to prohibit their entrance to the apparition site. The people, however, were not to be deterred. The fervor of the pilgrims' prayer and singing overwhelmed even the armed resistance, and all the soldiers threw down their rifles and joined in the prayerful procession that day.[18] The anti-religious fanatics weren't finished, however. The original chapel, built in 1920, was dynamited in March of 1922 in an attempt to destroy the growing Fatima devotion, but it was rebuilt a few years later, and the foundation stone of

17 Kaczmarek, *The Wonders She Performs*, 19.
18 Ibid., 123-24.

the larger shrine was laid in 1928.[19] In an act of divine irony, the atheistic government was driven out of power nine years after the apparitions without the least bloodshed; it was eventually replaced with a representative government run by António de Oliveira Salazar, who ruled as Prime Minister for more than three decades.[20] This first statue of Our Lady of Fatima remained permanently in the Sanctuary from 1920 onward and is still displayed for veneration in the little Chapel of the Apparitions at Fatima.

The custom of Marian processions began with this statue in 1942, the Silver Jubilee of the apparitions. To commemorate the anniversary, a "Girls' Catholic Youth Movement" that took place from April 8th through May 13th of that year organized the first procession ever from the Sanctuary of Fatima to Lisbon and back with Thedim's original statue being carried in procession.[21] This event established the tradition of processions for which Fatima is so famous, although the original Fatima statue was never intended to be a "pilgrim" statue as such; future statues would fulfill that purpose.

Four years later, on May 13th, 1946,[22] Thedim's original statue was crowned in Fatima by the Papal Legate, Cardinal Aloisio Masella, under the title of "Queen of the World" while His Holiness, Pope Pius XII, addressed a radio audience of 800,000 devotees at that same hour: "Your ardent love, full of gratitude led you here," spoke the Pontiff to the pilgrims at Fatima,

> and you wished to give a tangible form to this love by symbolically representing it in that precious crown, which is the fruit of much generosity and of many sacrifices with which we have now crowned the miraculous statue by means of our Cardinal Legate.[23]

This coronation was carried out in conjunction with the celebration of Portugal's third centenary of the proclamation of Our Lady of the Immaculate Conception as Patroness and Queen of the country. Our Lady's Queenship

19   Apostoli, *Fatima for Today*, 122.

20   Haffert, *Russia Converted*, 71 73.

21   Michele Braun, *Soul* Magazine, March-April, 1981.

22   The chronology and details of the coronation are taken from John Haffert, *There is Nothing More* (Washington, New Jersey: AMI Press, n.d.), 325, as well as from my inteview with Mr. Haffert at the Blue Army Headquarters on 4/27/99 hereafter referred to as the Haffert Interview of 4/27/99.

23   Ibid.

over Portugal was recognized by a public act of King João IV as far back as 1646. It was hardly a coincidence then, that in 1917 the Virgin Mary would personally visit a country that had been consecrated to Her.

In December of the same year the original statue went on pilgrimage again, this time to Lisbon for the feast of the Immaculate Conception. At one point during the procession to Lisbon, four white doves were released into the air and three of them settled on the statue's base at the feet of Our Lady's Statue and remained there for the rest of the two week trip without eating or drinking. In the Cathedral of Lisbon during the pilgrimage, two of the doves separated and flew to opposite sides of the sanctuary where they folded their wings in what looked like a gesture of adoration as the Bishop raised the consecrated Host. The third dove flew to the top of the statue and perched on the golden crown of the statue that had just been placed on Our Lady's sacred head in May of that year. Then, as the Bishop pronounced the "Ecce Agnus Dei" and held up the consecrated Host for the adoration of the faithful, the white dove spread its wings and held them open in another gesture of profound respect. These extraordinary events, collectively called "The Miracle of the Doves," are recorded in several independent sources.[24]

Were we to speak of any difficulty with the original statue, however, it is that it was *not made according to the observations of Sister Lucia,* the only living person who had ever actually seen Our Lady. Thedim's original statue was modeled largely after the statue of Our Lady of Lapa, an image which he had seen in a Portuguese religious catalog published in 1914.[25] He told John Haffert that he had created the image *prior to 1917* and then later adapted it to the general description of Our Lady of Fatima that he took from the well-known story.[26] As lovely as the original image was, however, there was need for a more faithful representation of the Virgin Mary as She appeared to the three shepherd children in the apparitions of 1917.

---

24 Haffert, *Russia Converted,* 188-97 – in Portugal; Francis Johnston, *Fatima, the Great Sign* (Charlotte: Tan Books, 2012), 124 – in Brazil; Jesús Marti Ballester, "Una Señora Más Brillante Que El Sol: La Virgen de Fátima," 5/13/09 – in Spain and France; http://www.ciberia.es/~jmarti/LA%20VIRGEN%20DE%20%20FATIMA.html.

25 João Gonçalves Gaspar, "A Capela E A Imagem Da Cova Da Iria," n.d.

26 Haffert, *Her Own Words,* 153.

The "European" Statue

In 1921, the remaining seer, Lucia, at the age of thirteen went to live at the Convent of Vilar in a suburb of Porto, Portugal. The convent was an orphanage directed by the Dorothean Sisters. She left Fatima at the request of the Bishop in order to be protected from the pious crowds and other less well-intentioned persons who were constantly hounding her for information or seeking the nostalgic feeling of meeting the only living person who had spoken to the Queen of Heaven. Even in the orphanage, she took an assumed name and no one but the Mother Superior knew who she was. It was here that she wrote her reflections on the apparitions at the insistence of the Bishop.

As she matured, Lucia felt attracted to the religious life and decided to join the Dorothean sisters who ran the orphanage that had been her home during those years. In 1925 and 1926, she went through the novitiate in Pontevedra and in Tuy, in Galicia, northern Spain. She received the habit on October 2nd, 1926. There she remained a novice between 1926 and 1928. She professed vows on October 3rd, 1928 remaining in the province of Galicia until 1946, when she moved to the House of Sardão in Vila Nova de Gaia, Portugal. On March 25th, 1948, the feast of Our Lady's Annunciation, she was transferred to the Carmel of Saint Theresa in Coimbra, Portugal and remained for the rest of her life a contemplative Carmelite nun.

In 1946 Lucia, then a consecrated nun, was allowed to visit the site of the apparitions for the first time since she left home in 1920. Although hard to imagine, Lucia had lived in a sort of exile for more than a quarter of a century from the place where Our Lady had appeared to her. On the day of her visit to her home, May 21st, 1946, Sr. Lucia entered the Sanctuary of the shrine incognito, undoubtedly feeling a deep nostalgia for the supernatural events that she witnessed there many years before. Apparently she was delighted to see that the Chapel of the Apparitions (which she had never seen) stood at the exact place where Our Lady had appeared to her.

She also took note of Thedim's original statue that was prominently displayed in the Sanctuary. Although she had seen pictures of the statue in various publications before and had even written to the Bishop in 1937 about the inconsistencies in numerous details to the vision of Our Lady. In her letter she commented, "On the holy cards I have seen, Our Lady appears to have two mantles. It seems to me that, if I knew how to paint, I still would not be capable to paint her as she is, I would only put on her the whitest possible tunic and suppress all adornments, except for a golden thread around her mantle." Among other things, Sr. Lucia noted that the original statue featured what she considered to be extraneous decorations, elaborate borders, and even an extra garment that did not accurately reflect Our Lady's vesture. She said that Our Lady had appeared with a golden globe on a chain around her neck, but not a tassel as the original statue showed.[27]

After her visit to the Sanctuary she spoke personally with the Bishop of Leiria-Fatima, Dom José Alves Correia da Silva (Fatima's Bishop from 1920-1957), about her concerns, repeating her observations, and it was then that the Bishop authorized an official study of the matter. The Bishop asked the statue's sculptor, José Ferreira Thedim, to speak with Sr. Lucia and make a new statue according to her description. The Bishop granted Thedim a face-to-face interview with the seer on November 9th, 1946, and the sculptor's brother, Guilherme, submitted an additional list of twenty-seven written questions for her to answer. Based on her answers, the sculptor made several sketches and returned to the convent for a second meeting. Sr. Lucia was still not satisfied with his work. Thedim then made a plaster model and met with the seer a third time. Sr. Lucia finally assented to the project but apparently was never fully satisfied with the result. With Sr. Lucia's approval, Thedim made a statue out of Brazilian cedar according to her guidelines; it was the first statue to be made from the seer's point of view. John Haffert believes that it was fashioned sometime in late 1946 or early 1947[28] and sent to the Bishop who housed it until he could bless it publicly on May 13th, 1947, the thirtieth anniversary of the first apparition.

On the day of the solemn blessing, 35,000 people attending the international Catholic Action Congress from five continents were making a pilgrimage to the Sanctuary, and they presented a resolution to the Bishop asking that a statue of Fatima *be taken on pilgrimage throughout Europe* with the ultimate goal of reaching Russia.[29] John Haffert notes that "Perhaps this

---

27 *Haffert,* Dear Bishop, 41.

28 As per the Haffert Interview of 4/27/99.

29 Haffert, Russia Converted, 199 and Her Own Words, 153.

Congress ... would long have been forgotten were it not for the resolution passed there that a statue of Our Lady should be carried in procession from Fatima to Russia."[30] We may call this statue the European statue for that reason. While this designation is not an official title, it is appropriate for the sake of distinguishing it from the others. When he received the petition, the Bishop consulted with Sr. Lucia about the idea of a traveling statue, and her response was very positive. She said, "Yes, Your Excellency," and added, "and let them take the statue which Thedim has made for you."

Soon after the blessing of May 13th, 1947, this new statue began to make pilgrimages throughout Europe and was immediately the occasion of many spectacular graces. For example, a priest from Charleroi, Belgium testified to John Haffert that on the occasion of the statue's visit to his parish, it was necessary to have *sixty-two priests* hearing confessions. Likewise, the statue's visit to Spain opened the long-closed border between Spain and France, a closure that pre-dated the Second World War. When, with thousands of faithful on both sides of the border singing the Fatima hymn, *Ave, Ave, Ave, Maria!* the local French and Spanish bishops met one another to transfer the statue. The border somehow miraculously opened to the statue and was never closed after that. These stories come from John Haffert's article on the various travelling statues in the November-December, 1947 edition of *The Scapular* magazine, written within a few months of the events themselves; they are thus a strong contemporaneous witness to them.

This statue returned to Fatima permanently in 1982[31] and was solemnly enthroned in the Basilica of Fatima on September 8th, 1985 (in honor of the 2000th anniversary of Our Lady's birth).[32] It remains on permanent display at the Sanctuary of Fatima to this day and is the statue which pilgrims normally see being carried through the crowds during the famous candlelight processions at the Sanctuary.

THE INTERNATIONAL PILGRIM VIRGIN STATUE

---

30   Haffert, Dear Bishop, 39.

31   According to Louis Kaczmarek, Wonders She Performs, 130.

32   Haffert, "The International Pilgrim Virgin," Soul Magazine, March-April 1986.

With the spectacular events surrounding the European statue, John Haffert perceptively understood that the Europeans would never allow the traveling European statue to leave their continent. He also correctly surmised that the statue wouldn't be allowed into Russia: it was just too potent a spiritual force. He then conceived of the idea of having two more statues made, one specifically for travel throughout North America, and another "covert" statue for Russia itself. He suggested this to the Bishop of Fatima as a way to resolve the initial impasse that had been created by the incredible popularity and public sensation that the European statue had caused. His idea was that this North American statue would travel throughout the United States and then make its way toward Russia from the direction of the East as the European one was doing the same from the West. Haffert's strategic mind was thinking of a holy pincer move against Soviet Russia using consecrated statues of Our Lady!

A generous benefactor named Mary Ryan of New York, offered to pay Mr. Haffert's expenses to travel to Portugal and present his proposal to the Bishop. Bishop Correia immediately accepted the idea and then wrote a letter that he could present to the sculptor Thedim concerning the making of two additional statues. The letter asked Thedim to treat the request as if it were made by the Bishop himself. The same Miss Ryan subsequently financed the two statues authorized by the Bishop. Incredibly, the artist who had sculpted the original statue in 1920 then carved three more statues of Our Lady of Fatima in a single year (1947): the European one and the two additional statues.

Thedim made the International Pilgrim Virgin Statue according to the same model he had used for the European statue, but the sculptor seemed to work with even greater care and attention to detail in carving the new Statue. For example, on the International Pilgrim Virgin Statue, Our Lady is shown with her mouth slightly open and teeth showing, which was a detail not incorporated into the European Statue. Such a fine detail only increased the Statue's beauty. Mr. Haffert remarked on his impression that Thedim made this Statue "with almost supernatural inspiration," that "he was doing something greater than artistry" and "with such labor that it is probably the most beautiful statue that was ever made."[33] I could not agree more with his assessment.

Mr. Haffert returned to Portugal for the solemn blessing of the two

33   Haffert Interview of 4/27/99.

additional statues made by Thedim on October 13th, 1947. At that ceremony, the Bishop crowned the statue that was destined for Russia but did not crown the Statue meant for North America because it would be crowned in America. More than two hundred thousand faithful participated in this solemn and historic event which Bishop José Correia da Silva explained was the first time a statue was blessed at Fatima, but not crowned. The wife of the U. S. Ambassador to Portugal, Mrs. John Wiley, was present as well and had the honor of holding the statue's crown. Following the ceremony the Pilgrim Virgin was transported to the airport in Lisbon by cars provided by the American Embassy. Despite being originally intended as a touring statue for North America, it quickly became known and identified as the "International Pilgrim Virgin Statue" because, from the very moment it left Fatima after the blessing, its travels have been international in character.

The International Pilgrim Virgin Statue is one of the most remarkable of all the Fatima statues. It stands only forty inches tall and weighs a mere thirty-three pounds, but its impact has been felt in over one hundred countries of the world, including the former Soviet Union, Communist China and numerous other countries that to this day remain dominated by atheistic Communism. So powerfully did this Statue of Our Lady of Fatima take the world by storm that by the end of Her very first tour (a forty-nine day tour of Canada and the United States in the Fall/Winter of 1947), Mary Ryan noted that "more than a million kisses had worn the paint completely" from one of the feet of the Statue.[34]

During the Statue's visit to the 1981 Eucharistic Congress held in Lourdes, France, Mr. Haffert arranged to have Her visit the Carmelite Convent in Coimbra, Portugal where Sr. Lucia lived out her life as a cloistered Carmelite nun. The overnight visit must have been a great consolation to the seer who had remarked that this Statue, of the various statues that had been made of the Fatima apparitions, was most faithful to the vision of the beautiful Lady who she had seen with her own eyes: "She [Sr. Lucia] remarked afterwards that she had never seen an image which so resembled the actual apparition of Our Lady," wrote John Haffert in his memoir of Sr. Lucia.[35] This

---

34   Mary Ryan, "200,000 Americans Welcome Their Queen," *The Scapular*, January-February, 1948, 5.

35   John M. Haffert, *To Shake the World: Life of John M. Haffert* (Asbury: The 101 Foundation, Inc., 2001), 87; Haffert, *Her Own Words*, 156;

was a remarkable admission given her observation in his 1946 interview with the seer that no image whatsoever could possibly capture the beauty of the Lady who appeared "all of light" (toda de luz in Portuguese): "We beheld a Lady all dressed in white. She was more brilliant than the sun and radiated a light more clear and intense than a crystal glass filled with sparkling water when the rays of the burning sun shine through it. She seemed to be made all of light and her garments also."[36]

This famous Statue of Our Lady of Fatima is perhaps the Pilgrim Virgin that more people in the world have seen than any other of the many Fatima statues. The remarkable Statue has been touring the world for seventy years and continues to be a most vibrant witness to the message and presence of Our Lady who wishes to lead the world to Christ and save it from self-destruction. This Statue, the International Pilgrim Virgin Statue, is the subject of this book.

THE "SECRET" STATUE FOR RUSSIA, THE FOURTH STATUE

The story of the "covert" statue for Russia is another tale of wonder. When the two statues were transported together to North America, the Pilgrim Virgin Statue immediately went on pilgrimage to Canada with its Custodians while John Haffert, with great discretion, took the crowned statue destined for Russia to a small chapel located on his farm in Washington, New Jersey, awaiting its chance to go to Russia. Today this is the site of the National Blue Army Shrine of Our Lady of Fatima, located in Washington, New Jersey. There it patiently awaited its opportunity to fulfill its mission – an unwitting casualty of Cold War politics.

In January of the Holy Year 1950, there occurred a change of priests at the American Embassy in Moscow which led to the fulfillment of Mr. Haffert's original desire for a Fatima presence at the core of the Communist empire. The change of priests was a result of the U.S. government's 1933 agreement with the Soviet regime which *technically* allowed a Catholic Chaplain to take up residence and minister to the spiritual needs of the American embassy staff and all other ex-patriots. This agreement was called the Roosevelt-Litvinov Agreement, which was not fully honored by the Russians until

36   Kaczmarek, Wonders She Performs, 128.

1950. It was the legal foundation for the Catholic Chaplaincy to Moscow, heroically administered by the Assumptionist Fathers from 1934-1999. Prior to 1950 the resident Catholic priest was allowed no public ministry whatsoever in Russia.

How this statue arrived in Moscow is almost unbelievable.[37] John Haffert happened to read in the newspapers about the assignment of the Assumptionist priest, Fr. Louis-Robert Brassard to the Catholic Chaplaincy, and when Father finally received his visa, Mr. Haffert met him in New York and transferred the statue to the priest for transport to Moscow.

A brief newspaper report on the granting of the visa did not go unnoticed. On December 23, 1949, Mr. John Haffert of the Ave Maria Institute, Asbury Park, New Jersey, wrote to Fr. Dufault [the Assumptionist Superior in Rome] saying that he had spoken by telephone to Fr. Brassard about one of the three replicas of the original statue of Our Lady of Fatima which had been blessed on October 13, 1949 [actually 1947], by the Bishop of Leiria, Portugal. Two of these statues, known as the "Pilgrim Virgins," were already being taken in procession throughout Europe and America as part of the crusade of prayer for the conversion of Russia.

The third statue, which Mr. Haffert himself had brought from Portugal, had hopefully been destined for Russia. Because there seemed to be little chance that it would ever get there, a shrine was being prepared for it in the United States. He was now offering it to Fr. Brassard who agreed to bring it with him to Moscow on condition that the fact not be publicized. Accepting the condition, Mr. Haffert explained that the twenty-pound statue could easily accompany Father's personal luggage. Thanking Mr. Haffert for his offer, Fr. Dufault concurred in the policy of silence.[38]

Letting go of that statue was one of the hardest things Mr. Haffert ever did: "It was like cutting off my arm," he said. But he also "gladly gave the statue because that was what it was for, to go to Moscow" he commented. Since Fr. Brassard was not technically a diplomat and therefore had no diplomatic

37   Story and quotes taken from my Haffert Interview of 4/27/99.

38   Robert J. Fortin, A.A., The Catholic Chaplaincy in Moscow: A Short History, 1934 -1999 (Brighton, Massachusetts: Assumptionist Fathers, 2004), 54.

rights or immunity, he brought the statue with him *not knowing how he was actually going to get it into Russia*. As luck (or rather, Providence) would have it, he was seated next to a Catholic diplomat on the same plane while traveling into Russia, and this man offered to place the statue in his personal luggage thereby granting it diplomatic immunity. Apparently, the crowned Fatima statue for Russia smuggled herself into Russia in such a clever way.

Fr. Brassard's tiny three-room apartment on Samovaya-Samotechnaya Street in Moscow must have reflected the poverty of the Nativity in a cave outside of Bethlehem. Our Lady's arrival there was so striking as to receive a mention in the history of the Catholic Chaplaincy to Moscow:

> In one room of his apartment, he had erected a makeshift altar with available packing cases and placed on it a dressed-up whiskey carton which served as a tabernacle. In a corner of the room, near the window, he enthroned the statue of Our Lady of Fatima, which he had brought with him and whose new home he described in a letter to the bishop of Leiria: "It is in my 8th-floor apartment that I offer the Holy Sacrifice under the loving smile of the Moscow Pilgrim Virgin. From that fortunate oratory, Our Lady dominates the city. In the distance, one can see the towers of the Kremlin. At night, when it is dark, the two luminous red stars which crown that building appear through the window, one on each side of Our Lady, like two lamps silently paying homage to the Queen."[39]

Indeed, John Haffert compared the lights from Red Square to "two vigil lights at the feet of the Queen who promised the conversion of Russia."[40] The mystery of Our Lady's love for Russia extended to all the faithful people who lived and worked there during the Communist era. It seems almost as if Our Lady *chose to go there* to accompany those who, amid increasing harassment and suffering, sought to keep the flame of faith alive in an atheistic system:

> The Chaplaincy was the religious center of gravity for those Catholics who were able to be in contact with it. It brought together people who

39   Ibid., 52-53.
40   Haffert, *Nothing More*, 46-47.

shared a belief in God, his Son and his Church, who looked to the Gospel to give value and direction to their lives, and who tried to live by Christ's message of love, knowing that it could transform the world and the society in which they lived into a more graced fellowship.

Given this bond of faith, those who frequented the chaplaincy were able to derive from it and from one another the support, encouragement and strength they needed to face the non-believing atheistic society that surrounded them. It was for them an oasis in the middle of the barren ideological desert that kept sapping their inner strength.[41]

The Assumptionist priests maintained the Catholic Chaplaincy for sixty-five years and were at times the only Catholic priests officially allowed to act in public in the Soviet Union. As difficult as it was, Fr. Brassard described his ministry as one of vital importance: "The situation could be very disheartening because, as yet, I have not been able to minister to my flock. Nevertheless, I feel that my mission is being accomplished even though it is not taking the shape that I would desire. Just my being here means that the Church is still alive."[42]

In October of 1992, after the fall of Communism, John Haffert made a pilgrimage to Moscow with the International Pilgrim Virgin Statue accompanied by two jumbo jets full of pilgrims (over nine hundred people), where they witnessed the reunion of the two statues that had been blessed at Fatima together forty-five years previously. The Vatican-appointed Apostolic Administrator for European Russia, Abp. Tadeusz Kondrusiewicz, arranged for the reunion of the two statues that year.[43] The Pilgrim Virgin Statue was crowned publicly in a ceremony presided over by a legate of the Bishop of Leiria-Fatima, and a fourteen-year-old Russian girl named Lena, a convert to the Catholic faith, placed the crown on Our Lady's head.[44] Most amazing of all was that the crowning took place in Red Square in front of the tomb of Vladimir Lenin.

---

41   Fortin, *Catholic Chaplaincy*, 129.

42   Ibid., 51.

43   Haffert, *Shake the World*, 137-38, 139.

44   Dan Lynch, *The Triumphant Queen of the World on Pilgrimage to Russia and China* (St. Alban's, Vermont: Missionary Image of Lady of Guadalupe, 1995), 24.

Various other "Pilgrim Virgin" statues

"National Pilgrim Virgin" statues have a long and fruitful role in the history of Fatima statues. The International Pilgrim Virgin Statue visited Vietnam in 1965, and as Mr. Haffert noted in his history of the Blue Army,

> the effect of the statue's tour was so great that the Vietnamese did not want it to leave their war-torn country. They pleaded that the statue remain until the hostilities were over. Unfortunately this was not possible, so they asked that a special statue be blessed for their country – and thus was born the idea of the "National Pilgrim Virgin."[45]

But that is not the total story of the Vietnamese statue. Pope Paul VI visited Fatima on May 13th, 1967 to commemorate the fiftieth anniversary of the apparitions, and on that occasion the Holy Father blessed twenty-five National Pilgrim Virgin statues that were destined to be personally delivered to various countries by the Bishop of Leiria-Fatima on an "Around the World Tour" with the Blue Army in the months following the Pope's visit. However, the Vietnamese people could not wait to receive their National Pilgrim Virgin statue. "[A] large Blue Army delegation came from Vietnam, going days without sleep, to be present [at the Pope's ceremony] and to carry that first National Pilgrim Virgin statue back with them at once to their suffering country."[46]

Another extraordinary blessing of statues took place on May 13th, 1971 – a simultaneous crowning of National Pilgrim Virgin statues around the world. In fact, the event was so momentous that John Haffert called it "perhaps the greatest manifestation in honor of the Blessed Virgin on a single day in history." Even Pope Paul VI participated in this event by sending a message through radio and television.[47] This event was organized to commemorate the twenty-fifth anniversary of the Coronation of the European statue by Pope Pius XII's Legate at Fatima. The 1971 blessing was conducted by the Cardinal Patriarch of Lisbon at the Sanctuary of Fatima before half

---

45   Haffert, *Dear Bishop*, 242-43.

46   Ibid.

47   John M. Haffert, The Brother and I (Washington, New Jersey: Ave Maria Institute, 1971), 190.

a million pilgrims while a further seventy replica National Pilgrim Virgin statues were concurrently crowned by bishops in many other countries of the world. The Cardinal blessed the same statue that had been venerated by Pope Paul VI on his visit in 1967, namely, the European statue, while John Haffert was in Moscow with a delegation of Blue Army members on that same day. They brought with them a crown for the statue of Russia that was in the custody of the American Embassy chaplain since 1950. The re-crowning of the Russian statue (which had originally been crowned in 1947) took place simultaneously with the blessings and crownings of the other seventy National Pilgrim Virgin statues.[48]

Incidentally, the National Pilgrim Virgin statue for the United States was blessed and crowned at the same time in the National Shrine of the Immaculate Conception by then-Archbishop of Washington D. C., Patrick Cardinal O'Boyle, and continues a generous travel schedule throughout the United States to this day. It is believed that the number of National Pilgrim Virgin statues today is approximately one hundred.

In addition to the National Pilgrim Virgin statues, a special Fatima statue was created and blessed for a specific mission to the United Nations in 1952. It was, for a brief time, displayed in the UN Meditation Room where Msgr. Colgan prayed the Rosary with a group of faithful on December 8th, the Solemnity of the Immaculate Conception, that year. This statue too has its own custodian and continues to make visitations to individual parishes upon request.[49]

To finalize the list, there are perhaps a few dozen copies of the famous and beloved International Pilgrim Virgin Statue replicas that have been created for veneration throughout the world. No single individual has a copyright on the beloved Statue or on devotion to Our Lady of Fatima – She is a gift to the Church and to the world! She wishes to be known as widely as possible, but more importantly, She wishes that Her message of conversion of heart be spread to the ends of the earth.

Our Statue for the world, the International Pilgrim Virgin Statue, has only one way by which She may travel the earth; that is, in the arms of Her faithful Custodians and beloved apostles of the Fatima message. As we exam-

48   Haffert, *Nothing More*, 47, 348.

49   http://wafusa.org/the-apostolate/national-pilgim-virgin-statue/.

ine the mission of this Statue for the conversion of the nations, we must look at the two men who I believe have done more to propagate the message of Fatima and "make straight the way" (Is 40:3; Jn 1:23) for the Pilgrim Virgin Statue than any other individuals on earth.

Two Great Apostles of Our Lady

Give me an army saying the Rosary and I will conquer the world.
~Pope Pius IX, 1792-1878.

his book is dedicated to two of the most extraordinary Marian apostles of our time: Mr. John Matthias Haffert and Professor Plinio Corrêa de Oliveira. These two faithful sons of Our Lady were contemporaries and peers in the mission of serving Holy Mother Church in the Twentieth Century. Although they never met, their roles in propagating the message of Fatima were unsurpassed during their lifetimes, each of which lasted more than eight decades. Not the least of their contributions to the Church and to humanity was their respective stewardship of the International Pilgrim Virgin Statue.[50]

I am aware of the daunting task of trying to summarize the lives and accomplishments of these two great men in so short a chapter, but I hope that these few pages will serve as a humble acknowledgement of their prophetic greatness for our age and a stimulus to the reader to discover more about two of Our Lady's great apostles of the 20th Century.

Our Lady's missionary

Anyone who ever met John Haffert – from Popes to the average lay parishioner – understood that he was a driven man. Mr. Haffert had, from his early

---

50 Stewardship implies governance and oversight, not necessarily an accompanying presence, much the way the Bishop of a diocese is the overseer of his flock but his priests are the pastors in individual parishes.

years felt a call to promote the Scapular of Our Lady of Mount Carmel as a way to sanctify the world, but he thought he would do it as a priest. After a period of discernment about whether or not to join the Carmelites, he understood that the priesthood was not his vocation as such. Rather, "union with Our Lady,"[51] was both his calling in life *and his mission*. As he was innately a man of action, he launched into the Scapular Apostolate under the auspices of the Carmelites of Western New York and began to publish *The Scapular* magazine. In his first few years as editor, the publication had a circulation of 163,000 subscriptions[52] and Mr. Haffert had achieved over one million Scapular enrollments for Our Lady, establishing himself in the proud tradition of the great Marian saints, like St. Maximillian Kolbe and St. Louis Marie de Montfort, in drawing souls to Christ through Mary.

John Haffert's two greatest sorrows came to him at the hands of Catholic clergy. He was dismissed from the Carmelites after three years in simple vows with no word of explanation except "God has not called you to this state."[53] It was painful for him not to be able to continue in religious life, but his dismissal also sowed the seeds of his future work. In 1948, Cardinal Spellman of New York obliged the Carmelites to place a priest in the position of editor of *The Scapular* magazine, which was something of a blow to Mr. Haffert's ambitions to conquer the world for Our Lady through that apostolate. Undaunted, in 1950 he launched Soul magazine as the official publication of The Blue Army, which he co-founded and incorporated in that same year with Msgr. Harold V. Colgan of the diocese of Camden, New Jersey, for the propagation of the Fatima message. Mr. Haffert succeeded in building *Soul's* readership to more than a quarter of a million subscribers by the time of his retirement as editor in 1987.

We have spoken already of Mr. Haffert's role in the concept and creation of the Pilgrim Virgin Statue, but prior to that, in 1946, he had the marvelous opportunity to conduct a personal interview with the lone living seer of Fatima, Sr. Lucia dos Santos. His four-hour meeting with Sr. Lucia must have had a singular impact upon his soul. He later recounted what grace he derived from the experience:

---

51   Haffert, *Brother and I*, 5.

52   Haffert, *Dear Bishop*, 38.

53   Haffert, *Brother and I*, 42.

If I were to summarize the goal of my life from the time in 1946, when I experienced the reality of Fatima after a long interview with Sister Lucia, I would describe it as a constant effort to shake the world by the shoulders and say: "Wake up! God has given us the specific response to save mankind from self-destruction!"[54]

When I read such a vibrant statement of a man's self-concept and life's work, I stand in deep awe of the blessing that was his life. There must be a special place in Heaven for those who dedicate themselves to the salvation of others with such fervor. Mr. Haffert in fact gave his life, all his material resources, and his best years for the salvation of the entire world and would never have claimed any credit for his six decades in the mission field. He was an extraordinary man whose accomplishments should be recognized for what they were: truly heroic.

After his meeting with Sr. Lucia, he was moved to transform the Scapular ministry into a larger campaign called the March for Pledges, in which the adherents pledged to consecrate themselves to Our Lady through the means of sanctification recommended at Fatima: the Five First Saturdays devotion (at first optional), the wearing of the Scapular, the daily Rosary, and the daily offering of the sacrifices of one's state in life as penance for the sins and sacrileges committed against the Immaculate Heart of Mary. The March for Pledges was eventually re-named "the Blue Army Pledge" and carried to the ends of the earth by the members of the Blue Army. It is estimated that the campaign produced anywhere between thirty and forty million pledges during the time it was carried out.[55]

Another one of the channels for Mr. Haffert's prodigious energy was his ministry of the word. Like his saintly predecessors St. Maximillian Kolbe and St. Louis Marie de Montfort, he educated the faithful by publishing his every thought on Our Lady's role and message in the salvation of souls. In fact, his literary accomplishments were extraordinary and would have impressed those same prolific Marian saints: thirty-two books, two publishing companies, three international publications (*The Scapular*, *Soul*, and *The Voice of the Two Hearts*; *Soul* magazine remains in publication after sixty years), as

54 Haffert, *Shake the World*, 58.

55 Source: http://wafusa.org/our-founders-history/.

well as hundreds of articles, promotional materials, talks, and conferences. Mr. Haffert also sponsored several "seminars of world-class theologians, and seminars for leaders" at Fatima.[56]

But John Haffert was not just an inspirational writer and publisher. His drive to bring people to Christ through Our Lady also burst out in numerous creative ways particular to the modern age. In the Fifties and Sixties he conducted innumerable radio and press interviews and sponsored a television show promoting the Fatima message that ran on over one hundred television stations, one episode of which featured then-Senator John F. Kennedy. He even produced a full-length motion picture about Fatima.[57] By way of his "Russia Will Be Converted" talks in parishes around the United States and in other parts of the world, he personally presented the message to tens of thousands of souls.

Adding to his immense repertoire of accomplishments, John Haffert was both a founder and a builder. We mentioned his role in the co-founding of the Blue Army with Msgr. Colgan. He set up and housed his budding apostolate in a converted barn on his farm in Washington, New Jersey in the early 1950s. In 1949 the barn became the Ave Maria Institute, which was later converted into the Blue Army offices.[58] In 1978 Mr. Haffert and his companions built the National Blue Army Shrine of Our Lady of Fatima which stands on the same property, which he generously donated to the organization. In 1951 he was the driving force for the construction of the Blue Army International Center (now called *Domus Pacis*, House of Peace), which became the first guest house and international pilgrim center near the Sanctuary in Fatima, Portugal. In 1972 he was the prime mover for the purchase and renovation of the convents in Pontevedra and Tuy, Spain wherein Sr. Lucia experienced personal apparitions of Our Lady in 1920s.[59]

Most importantly, when Our Lady prophesied that Russia would "spread its errors" throughout the world, John Haffert took it as a call to arms. He knew that these errors had already entered the world through athe-

---

56   Haffert, *Shake the World*, 58.

57   Ibid., 59 (Kennedy) and 45 (motion picture). All subsequent facts about Mr. Haffert's travels are from Chapter 6, "Travel," of this same book.

58   *Dear Bishop*, 82, 90-91.

59   Ibid., chs. 23-24.

istic Communism and were corrupting culture to the point of the loss of souls. He was an implacable foe of the Red Menace all his life and was full of zeal to save people from spiritual destruction. In this he was Our Lady's most ardent missionary: "It seems that I was almost breathlessly crying, over and over: 'Here is Heaven's specific response to save mankind from self-destruction!'"[60] he once wrote. He authentically believed that his Blue Army was the fulfillment of the message of Our Lady of Fatima.[61] The Blue Army (now titled the World Apostolate of Fatima) today has affiliates in twenty-five countries and seventy-seven dioceses throughout the world.

Yet, Mr. Haffert also understood that a political system like Communism was not the real enemy of the human race. Mankind's enemy was *atheism*, the vision that humanity had no need of God. He understood that the men and women of the Twentieth Century were involved in an epic spiritual battle that could only be won with spiritual weapons and the heroic faith of believers:

> The great issue at stake now is between God and anti-God, between the Light and the Darkness. Darkness has always tried to overcome the light, but the crisis of our times rose from the great armed might and international union of the Darkness against the Light...and the feeble faith of the Light-bearers.[62]

Our Lady's most effective missionary took in Her urgent message and believed, with all his heart, that the war for souls could only be won "on our knees." (Ibid.)

Mr. Haffert's pioneering vision conceived of the idea of a traveling statue of Our Lady of Fatima and confirmed him as one of Her great apostles. It is hardly surprising, therefore, that he was blessed to have the Statue by his side in the last several months of his life. In my 2013 interview with John's wife, Patricia Haffert, she spoke of his love for Our Lady and of the remarkable synchronization of his life with the travels of the Statue:

---

60   Haffert, *Shake the World*, 58.

61   Haffert, *Dear Bishop*, 30.

62   Haffert, *Russia Converted*, 144.

I would say that John had a special attachment...a special devotion. He always said it was only a wooden statue but that there was a special grace attached to it. I can remember on one occasion he received a letter from a person who was an atheist. He had written the letter to John to say that he had come into contact with the Pilgrim Virgin Statue and was inspired by it. So much so that it led to his conversion to the Catholic Faith.

John always saw the statue as an instrument to spread the message Our Lady gave at Fatima and through the many, many pilgrimages around the world with the statue, the message was brought to people far and wide.

On our 25th wedding anniversary in 2001 we did not know if the IPVS was in the area but John had contact with the custodian Carl Malburg and it just so happened that he was going to be close by with the statue that day. On May 1st, 2001 the statue came to our house. John always had a very special attachment to this statue. On that occasion when the statue arrived John went with Carl and took the statue to every room throughout the house which we had built four years earlier. We considered it a very special grace to have the statue here on our 25th anniversary because John passed away just five months later in October of that year.

Mrs. Haffert further recounted the touching story of John's final days. Was it a coincidence that the Pilgrim Virgin Statue, frequently on pilgrimage in foreign countries, was within two hours' drive of the Hafferts' home at that time?

John was really a very down to earth person. I recall the last few days that John was in the intensive care unit dying of cancer; he asked me if I could find out if it would be possible for him to have a visit of the IPVS so that he could see her one last time. I looked into it and learned that by chance the statue was free and that she could be brought to the hospital. It is not normal to bring statues into the hospital so I asked the doctor if that would be alright and he said yes. So for the last days of his life the statue stood at the foot of his bed. During those final days in the hospital we prayed the three rosaries together every day as was John's custom. John was wearing an oxygen mask so he could not respond but he accompanied the rosary with his beads. I recall that frequently he would cast his gaze at the statue. The statue was with him when he passed away [on October 31st, 2001.]

Mr. Haffert's wake and funeral took place on the grounds of the World Apostolate of Fatima's national headquarters. The wake was in the chapel of the Holy House the night before, in the presence of the Pilgrim Virgin Statue, and the next day his casket was carried in procession across the grounds to the outdoor chapel for the funeral Mass. The Pilgrim Virgin led the procession while a line of family, friends and dignitaries followed. I felt blessed to have been asked to be one of the pallbearers to carry the coffin. The Pilgrim Virgin was placed near the altar and was present during the funeral. Our Lady was there to bid farewell to a faithful son.

OUR LADY'S PROPHET

A prophet is not prophetic because he has a clairvoyant ability to tell the future, he is a prophet because he is able to clearly discern the looming consequences of present behaviors. Moreover, his clear-eyed willingness to speak truth to power inevitably places him in direct confrontation with those whose behaviors are leading souls or societies – or both – to destruction. We can observe this throughout the course of history. While other men can shrug off the thought of the doom that awaits them and ignore the pending chastisement for their wickedness, the prophet cannot. He must speak the truth despite the cost. Sight, speech, and sacrifice are a prophet's stock and trade, and Dr. Plinio Corrêa de Oliveira knew each of these in abundance.

There is an inspiring story about Dr. Plinio when he was just four years old that expresses his life-long fervor for the Church. On a sojourn in Europe with his family, little Plinio attended a puppet show in the Théâtre des Marionettes in Paris where, in the typical anti-clerical spirit of the French, he witnessed an "alligator" puppet poised to eat a "priest" puppet in the play. The four-year-old boy immediately stood on the chair, raised his small hand, and in perfect French disputed with the puppeteers: "No, it's not true! He is a priest, it's not right!"[63] If the child Plinio had any preparation for his vocation of service to the truth, it was more by grace than by nature, although he did always credit his saintly mother, Doña Lucilia, with a consistent formation in virtue and faith, and in fidelity to the Church that were hallmarks of Dr. Plinio's mission throughout his life.

His love of Our Lady was deep and ardent. A few years after the puppet incident, young Plinio was caught in an innocent deception that caused his mother to wonder out loud if she should send him to a boarding school far away from home. The very thought of separation from his family struck fear in the heart of the boy. When he later visited his local parish, he knelt in front of the church's statue of Our Lady Help of Christians, and pleaded with the Virgin, "Save me, Oh Queen!" His internal state of desperation soon gave way to a profound, penetrating peace which made him understand that the Blessed Mother would resolve everything in his favor and save him from the worst consequences of his own behavior. Although the profound experience did not include a vision or apparition, it reminds us of the moment in which young Raymond Kolbe (the future St. Maximillian) turned to Our Lady for solace when his mother scolded him. The results of the two encounters were the same: profound peace of soul and a deep understanding of his "belong-ingness" to the Queen of Heaven,[64] which marked his life and mission with an indelible seal.

Dr. Plinio's brilliance and goodness was evident in every aspect of his life, from his dedication to the preservation of truly Catholic culture in his native Brazil (which is the largest Catholic country in the world) to his astounding career as a journalist and public servant. As a teenager he joined the large Catholic popular movement called the Marian Congregation; he would eventually become its national director. He was a nationally known Catholic speaker by his early twenties and because of his renown as a dynamic Catholic, he was promoted by the Archbishop of Sao Paulo as the Catholic coalition candidate to the national Constitutional Assembly at the age of 24. This fact alone shows how mature in intellect, piety, and human virtue young Plinio was for his age; the promotion of such a young man for public

63   This delightful story is told by Andrea F. Phillips in her excellent cameo biography, *Plinio: A Man for Our Times* (Spring Grove: The American Society for Tradition, Family, and Property, 2010), 11.

64   Phillips, *Plinio*, 28-29.

office was unprecedented in Brazil at the time. In fact, he was the youngest congressman ever elected to the Constitutional Assembly and received more votes than any other congressman in Brazil, more than twice as many as the nearest competitor.

In 1933 he was asked by the Archbishop of Sao Paulo to become the editor of *O Legionário*, the largest Catholic weekly newspaper in Brazil, and in that position he became a clarion voice for Catholic orthodoxy and culture. Nonetheless, he was rejected for many of his orthodox stances and also *ignored*, perhaps a more effective tactic of his enemies to try to minimize his influence. But Dr. Plinio was never deterred or cowered by opposition and he conveyed that to his allies. This courage and resilience was very clearly marked by his profound devotion to the Blessed Virgin Mary. I recall a verse from the official hymn of the Marian Congregation that he liked to cite as an example of the degree of confidence we need to have in Our Lady: *A thousand swords scare not the soldier / Who in Thy shadow fights, Immaculate!*

In 1943 he wrote a book denouncing the liberalizing forces that were infiltrating the Catholic Church and other groups such as the powerful Catholic Action, an organization that he headed. That publication proved to be a watershed moment in his life. He was immediately fired from his position as editor of *O Legionário* and lost virtually every close associate that he had worked with for the past several decades. Some of his closest collaborators turned against him in the blink of an eye, ostracizing him from every group and association that he had belonged to prior to the publication of the book. Faithful servants who dare speak the truth of their convictions very rarely live comfortable lives. His observations about the modernist ideas and trends in the areas of fashion, doctrine, and discipline, however, have all been borne out by subsequent changes in Church and society. The suffering of these years of isolation would later produce great fruit in a spiritual sense with the founding of the Society for The Defense of Tradition, Family, and Property (TFP) movement, which he would establish in 1960 with a small cadre of faithful friends.[65] All the while, he never lacked confidence and his devotion to his Heavenly Mother grew more ardent.

65   Ibid., 130-31.

Though grounded in the Divine Magisterium of the Catholic Church and drawing their inspiration from her teachings, the TFPs were established as "lay apostles" in direct response to Dr. Plinio's inner call to work for the interest of the Church and Christian Civilization in the world.[66]

`The TFP soon after expanded to many other countries and resulted in the establishment of many sister organizations. In 1951, he founded the publication Catolicismo which became the vehicle through which he would continue to offer his insights and influential opinions on the state of the Church and the world.

DR. PLINIO'S WORLDVIEW

Dr. Plinio observed and addressed what he called the process of *Revolution* in history, by which he meant the cumulative force of mankind's rebellion against God, having its taproot in the original revolt of Lucifer and the fallen angels. His epic work on this subject, written in 1960, is entitled *Revolution and Counter-Revolution*;[67] it is his most famous and influential work. It is not my purpose to outline the fullness of his thought in these pages, but to summarize how his perceptions dovetail perfectly with the meaning he found in the apparitions of Fatima.

In his book, Dr. Plinio very clearly outlined the roots of the profound decadence of Western civilization. The period of the Middle Ages was the height of the union of Catholic teaching with Christian culture, a civilization that had developed over many centuries and was understood as the beautiful fruit of so many saints and scholars. But since the 14th Century Western civilization began a long, slow decline through a series of violent revolutions that took aim at the synthesis of faith and reason that had ruled the day in the Middle Ages. The decline began with the Protestant Reformation (16th Century) which was a *religious* rebellion. It continued in the French Revolu-

---

66   Ibid., 116.

67   Plinio Corrêa de Oliveira. *Revolution and Counter-Revolution.* York: American Society for the Defense of Tradition, Family and Property, 1993.

tion (18th Century), which was a *political* rebellion; and in a much more radical and bloody way, the decline reached its culmination in the Communist Revolution (20th Century), which had the characteristic of a *socioeconomic* rebellion foretold by Our Lady at Fatima.

Communism, Dr. Plinio wrote, "burst forth from the increasingly ardent spirit of the Revolution"[68] as if it were an "immense avalanche"[69] of evil that modern man finds impossible to control and that is sweeping souls away to destruction. Building upon the "avalanche" analogy, if we understand the various rebellions as a spiritual wave that gradually builds force over the centuries, the 20th Century was the point at which the Revolution's tidal wave of evil crested and began to wash onto the shores of humanity. It was also at this very point that Our Lady appeared at Fatima to bring Her strong warning to the world.

In 1960 Dr. Plinio described in his masterful book, *Revolution and Counter-Revolution*, a coming fourth revolution, which today we would call the *Cultural* Revolution; but he did not attempt to describe that revolution in detail because, like Our Lady of Fatima, he left room for human free will to determine the future. With these insights, however, Dr. Plinio saw that Our Lady's concern for sinful humanity confirmed all that he had previously taught and understood about modernism and the evils of Communism. His outlook completely fit together with Our Lady's message of Fatima. In fact, he believed that the plan of Fatima could defeat the Revolution, which is why he became such an ardent Fatima apostle. Andrea Phillips notes that Dr. Plinio was "a living, attentive witness of the truth of Our Lady's prophetic words" at Fatima.[70]

OUR LADY'S TWO GREAT APOSTLES
IN THE COMMUNION OF SAINTS

It is no surprise, then, that when John Haffert was asked to send the International Pilgrim Virgin Statue on pilgrimage to Latin America in the mid-Sev-

68 Ibid., 18.
69 Ibid., 4.
70 Ibid., 95.

enties he was confident in entrusting it to the willing organizer and overseer in the person of Dr. Plinio and his TFP organizations, which had spread to at least six other countries of Latin America and numerous others in Europe and North America by this time.[71] Dr. Plinio had, of course, been aware of the Fatima event and message for many years, but it was only after the first and second parts of the message were revealed to the world in 1941 that he, as well as many other Catholics, understood Fatima as a message for the whole of humanity.

When he read about the weeping statue in 1972 in a major Brazilian newspaper, he had his TFP representatives contact John Haffert in the US about the prospect of the Statue visiting South America. He offered his network to be stewards of the Statue for Latin America. He welcomed the Pilgrim Virgin Statue to Brazil for the first time in May of 1973 and then sponsored Her near decade-long pilgrimage throughout Latin America beginning in July of 1974.[72] In subsequent chapters we will recount many of the marvelous stories and wonders that took place as a result of Our Lady's pilgrimage to the most Catholic of continents. It is thanks to the vigor and virtue of the two great apostles of Fatima, John Haffert and Plinio Corrêa de Oliveira, that the people of the whole world have been able to bask in the presence of Her enchanting gaze.

Our Lady chose and formed Her two witnesses well: both men were articulate orators, writers, and publishers; both men formed pious societies as instruments through which they could incorporate others into the saving mission; both were warriors and men of action and, as a result, suffered deeply for their convictions. They were both stalwart foes of atheistic Communism in an era when the menace of that pernicious ideology was the highest.[73] Not surprisingly, Mr. Haffert chose blue for his army to mirror Our Lady's color and to symbolically counter the forces of the Red Menace. Dr. Plinio's forces, in contrast, have always worn a sash of deep crimson in their activities to signify the blood of the martyrs and combat for the faith. Above all, both were men of the Church, living a life of grace and dependent upon the strength of God to accomplish all they achieved.

---

71   Phillips, *Plinio*, 115.

72   This is the chronology given by Phillips, *Plinio*, 154.

73   Phillips, *Plinio*, 134.

That is why I found it to be very timely and opportune to be by Mr. Haffert's bedside several weeks before he died. Our brief time together that evening manifested the almost mystical link between the two great apostles of Fatima in a way that I could never have anticipated; and of course, the uniting element between the two was Fatima and the Pilgrim Virgin Statue. Mr. Haffert had been suffering from cancer (and the effects of chemotherapy and radiation) for many months prior to his death on October 31st, 2001, but the cancer had taken a turn for the worse and he asked me to come see him in the nursing home where he was spending his last days. As he was putting his affairs in order the one thing that preoccupied him most was the future of the wonderful Statue that he had brought into the world more than fifty years earlier. He personally owned the Statue but did not have a plan for how it would be utilized after his death. None of the various apostolates that he had been associated with during his long career were in charge of it, and he feared that there could be confusion about the Statue's future mission when he was gone. He wanted the Statue to be a cause of union among them, not a cause of division.

In those years I served as the vice president of Tradition, Family and Property and their America Needs Fatima campaign, and in the course of our two hours together I felt that I helped console him as to any concern he had about the stewardship of the Statue. We had built a solid relationship over the years so it was not surprising that he wanted to express to me his concern and desire that the TFP and the Blue Army both be involved with the Statue's apostolate. I gave Mr. Haffert some perspective about how long he had actually been involved, unofficially, with the TFP and their network and various resources throughout the world. For example, when the Statue needed restoration in 1977, the TFP marshalled the talents of the best restorers in Europe to renew the Statue's incredible beauty. It was also a TFP artist who restored the hands of the statue when they were broken after its sojourn in Australia and carried out a complete restoration in 1999. I explained to him how much the TFP network throughout the world had done to promote the message of Fatima through the visits of the Pilgrim Virgin Statue, and after a while it was evident to him that he had really been working with the TFP and promoting Fatima through the Statue for many years. I'm sure that he had understood that during the times he sent the Statue to Dr. Plinio in

Latin America – always receiving it back on time and in excellent shape as he recalled to me on many occasions – but at this moment he was able to appreciate his alliance with Dr. Plinio in a new way. It was a true moment of grace and enlightenment which brought a profound sense of peace to him.

As if sensing the presence of Our Lady with us then, I suggested that we pray and leave the whole matter of the Pilgrim Virgin Statue in God's hands. With amazing insight, Mr. Haffert said to me, "Thomas, you told me that Dr. Plinio was a lawyer, and I am sure he would appreciate our making this appeal. Why don't we pray three Hail Mary's asking Dr. Plinio to intercede and help us with this situation – to make everything work out alright?" I was deeply touched by his sentiment and the sense of mystical union that he had at that moment with the great apostle of Our Lady who had preceded him to his eternal reward some six years earlier. I believe our Catechism calls that the communion of saints.

With our humble and simple prayer in union with Dr. Plinio, it seemed like Our Lady had come down to meet us in that room with Her profound peace and to allay any concern we might have had about the future of the Pilgrim Virgin Statue. In fact, my main goal was to show Mr. Haffert that what he wanted (care of the Statue for the future) was actually happening – and Dr. Plinio was part of that plan as much in death as he was in life.

OUR LADY CLAIMS HER DOMINION

*In 1946 we crowned Our Lady of Fatima as Queen of the world,
and the next year, through her pilgrim image, She set forth as though to
claim Her dominion, and the miracles She performs along the way are
such that we can scarcely believe our eyes at what we are seeing.*
~Radio address of Pope Pius XII on May 13th, 1951.[74]

A person who has an official ambassador is undoubtedly someone to listen to; but a person who has a *Queen* as an ambassador is someone to be obeyed without question.

Any discussion of Our Lady's role in salvation history must take into account Her exalted dignity as "Queen of the world," as His Holiness, Pope Pius XII called Her. Her role as Queen even surpasses this world. The Book of Revelation (12:1-11) pictures Her as a woman clothed with the celestial elements and bearing a crown of stars on Her head as She gives birth to the Son who would rule over all of human history. As Queen, She has total rights over the created order and a preeminent authority over the realm of grace. She bears the divine authority of Her Son wherever She goes, and that is why She may go anywhere She wishes.

When I interviewed John Haffert in 1999 at the Blue Army Headquarters,[75] he pointed out something that the Bishop of Leiria-Fatima said to

---

74   In this radio address Pope Pius XII cited the crowning of a different Fatima statue, the precursor of the Statue which is the subject of this book. However, he was referring in a more generalized way to the immense graces that resulted from the travels of the various Fatima statues, particularly those marvels surrounding the International Pilgrim Virgin Statue which were already in great evidence by the early Fifties when he gave his address.

75   Haffert Interview of 4/27/99.

him some years later when the Bishop was told that a certain priest Custodian had taken the Statue on a different itinerary than the planned one. The priest had in fact left the official Custodian of the Statue behind. The wise Bishop thought about the situation for a few seconds and commented solemnly, "Let Our Lady go where She wills." Mr. Haffert took that insight from a saintly man to be a sort of paradigm for how Our Lady Herself determines where She wishes to go in this world to save souls. She seems to continuously go forth to "claim Her dominion," and whenever we "let Her go where She wills," She performs wonders.

OUR LADY'S PRESENCE OPENS THE WAY TO CHRIST

John Haffert's travels with the Statue are legendary. In them he often experienced Our Lady's ability to open doors to Christ's life-giving message. In the tens of thousands of miles that he traveled with the Pilgrim Virgin Statue, he regularly encountered problems, some of which were of a structural nature like unforeseen changes in schedule or lack of resources. At other times, the problems were related to human situations like unreasonable attitudes, ill will, rules, regulations, lack of access, or blockages that needed to be overcome for Her to reach more people. Whatever the situation, problem, or dilemma, he noticed that Our Lady always seemed to work things out and to create an even more favorable environment for the preaching of the Gospel message of conversion than if the problem had never existed in the first place.

Mr. Haffert tells the story of the Statue's visit to Czechoslovakia during Communist times.[76] He led 107 pilgrims on an around-the-world tour to deliver twenty-five copies of the Pilgrim Virgin Statue to numerous different nations, statues that had been blessed by the Holy Father, Pope Paul VI, during his pontifical visit to Fatima in May of 1967. The flight to Prague was Mr. Haffert's first attempt to bring a statue of the Pilgrim Virgin into a Communist country, but when the steel of Our Lady's desire for souls came into contact with the Iron Curtain, sparks began to fly. The story is very instructive about Our Lady's ability to open the way to the

76   Haffert, *Dear Bishop*, 244-48.

message of peace and repentance.[77]

The year was 1967, and, Mr. Haffert had publicized this tour behind enemy lines as a "peace flight," a concept that no one could take exception to – or so he thought. The Communists were very wary of Mr. Haffert's Fatima mission however. An article in the 1967 Communist publication, *Science and Religion*, was highly critical of the Blue Army and singled it out as one of the most potent forces combatting organized Communism throughout the world.[78] For this reason, he was quite amazed that the Communist authorities had allowed the Statue into the country at all. Nonetheless, he was immediately reminded of Our Lady's presence and power upon arrival. "When we landed at Prague airport," he recounts, "there was not a soul in sight. But an absolutely perfect and complete rainbow appeared over the airport … beginning and ending on the tarmac."[79] All the pilgrims saw the rainbow as an immense sign of favor upon their journey.

Nevertheless, after their peaceful arrival, the pilgrim group encountered the Communists' highly effective but subtle harassment as they attempted to get through passport control. Mr. Haffert apparently "had not counted on the malicious shrewdness of the Communists."

> I did not suspect that anything was wrong until our visas were being examined one by one, so painstakingly that our people were standing in line two hours after the plane had landed – even though there was no one else in the air terminal and the visas were all in order.
>
> I then began to shout in a loud voice that our buses were waiting, and that…they should at least allow those who had already cleared the formalities to board the coach.
>
> My shouting made no difference.[80]

Another (spiritual) force did make a difference, however. Suddenly, a white-haired man in a distinctive uniform came over and asked Mr. Haffert about the curious blue pin on his lapel. He explained that it was the insignia

---

77   Haffert, *Dear Bishop*, 243-48.

78   Ibid., 276-77.

79   Ibid., 245.

80   Ibid.

of the group that had come to pray for peace. *Inexplicably*, the white-haired official then motioned to another man with a wave of his hand – all the formalities immediately ceased, and the group was released to the buses! Mr. Haffert found out later that the official was actually a "person of high authority" who had the power to open the way for the pilgrim group with the wave of his hand.

Did Our Lady soften the heart of that Communist operative? Perhaps, and perhaps not. What She certainly did was to use a human decision, the act of a human mind and will, to open the way to those who were praying for peace and conversion. We must recognize the true futility of human efforts when confronting an organized spiritual force of evil such as the atheistic system that enslaved whole nations behind the Iron Curtain for decades. Merely human efforts were often powerless to penetrate it. Despite Mr. Haffert's attempts to force entrance into the country, Our Lady easily opened the way for the pilgrims so that thousands could hear the message of Fatima in a completely Communist-controlled country. In the end, Our Lady rewarded the courage of the pilgrims who were bringing the message of the Gospel to Communist lands. She worked everything out just perfectly.

After they were released for travel in the country, the pilgrim group soon met the Archbishop of Prague, Franeizek Cardinal Tomasek, who told them that he thought every Catholic household in Czechoslovakia prayed the Rosary for the fulfillment of Our Lady of Fatima's promises. Would that the whole world did the same! The pilgrims dutifully delivered the replica statue in Prague as Czechoslovakia's own "National Pilgrim Virgin," and the Archbishop exclaimed with a full heart, "You have brought us the sign of our Hope."[81]

John Haffert also noted that only a few months after the Statue's visit to that totalitarian state, Czechoslovakia made a bid for religious freedom that embarrassed the Soviets and perhaps, ultimately, lit a wildfire that burned deeply under the surface of the godless system, a blaze that eventually melted the Iron Curtain two decades later. Without overstating our claims, we can certainly surmise that Our Lady had something to do with the eventual dissolution of the whole Soviet order in time.

81   Haffert, *Brother and I*, 212.

Release from a Communist "Prison" of Sorts

Our Lady's opening power is unlimited, and She manifests it where She wills. In December of 1983 then-Custodian of the Pilgrim Virgin Statue, Mr. Louis Kaczmarek, had a similar, if not even more remarkable experience of Our Lady's power to open a door. In this case it was a door *out of* a Communist country. Kaczmarek had brought the Statue to the Marxist dictatorship of Zimbabwe in southern Africa where the Statue held a one-night vigil in the church of the Immaculate Conception in the capital city of Harare. Entering the country was easy, he said, "but leaving it was like a fly trying to escape a spider's web!"[82] Kaczmarek went on to recount how difficult it was to pass through the standard check points at the airport.

Seeing an opportunity to extort money from an American tourist, the armed guards rifled through his luggage, frisked him convict-style, harassed him, and demanded an enormous sum of money for the simple act of exiting a country. Kaczmarek resisted and bickered with the guards for some time, but they eventually threatened him with imprisonment if he didn't pay up. He could see no realistic way out of this dilemma because he didn't have the money. Neither did he wish to incur the fate of other tourists who had been kept in Communist jails for months in similar situations. Then Our Lady acted.

> My concern could not have been greater when, out of nowhere, a Catholic priest came to my rescue and dished out a good tongue lashing to the guards for their treatment of me. Strangely, the guards said nothing. I was wondering if this was St. John the Baptist, or St. John the Evangelist … or maybe even St. Joseph? The priest disappeared almost like a vapor as I ran, statue in arms, to catch the plane which was already winding up its engines…. The two hour flight to Johannesburg, South Africa, was filled with prayers for the captive people in the communist nations, with intermittent thoughts of that priest who had rescued me. Surely, Our Lady had sent him. (Ibid.)

82 Kaczmarek, *Wonders She Performs*, 136-37.

Apparently, even Marxist Zimbabwe belongs to Our Lady.

A FALLEN-AWAY CATHOLIC RENEWED

It is unanimously agreed upon by the Custodians of the Statue over the past seventy years that the greatest miracle performed by Our Lady is the conversion of a soul. If anything can be called Her "dominion" it is the reign of love that She has over the human soul. She is especially effective in bringing back those who have abandoned the Faith and in inspiring those who have no faith at all. For example, the Statue went on pilgrimage to St. Paul, Minnesota in 1983 where a self-described lukewarm Catholic named Connie Schneider attended the prayer service. She and her husband had been away from the sacraments for many years, but it took only one encounter with the enchanting gaze of the Virgin Mary for Connie's faith to be instantly renewed. On a visit of the Statue to her hometown some twenty years later, she gave an interview to a reporter about that life-changing experience:

> [Connie] still has a hard time explaining the deep connection made that day, but she walked away with the feeling a maternal spirit was watching over her, encouraging her to re-open her heart.
>
> "That statue, there's something special about it," she said. "A spiritual experience is different for everyone. But for me, when you have an experience like that, you feel like you're the only person in the entire universe that the mother of God is paying attention to. And that," she said, "is how it really, really is."[83]

There is nothing more special to a child than the undivided attention of his mother. Connie felt Our Lady's powerful gaze imprinting itself on her interior life, and decades later the glow of that encounter with Our Lady's grace was still fresh in her mind and heart. More importantly, twenty years after the event Connie had remained "a devout Catholic ever since." (Ibid.) I have said many times – and experiences like these make it abundantly clear to me – that whenever we experience challenges or difficulties of any type, we

83   Rex W. Huppke, "Statue and its caretaker make journeys of faith," *Chicago Tribune*, 3/25/04.

need only to turn to God's Mother and Our Lady will work everything out for us. We only have to place all our cares, concerns, and even our seemingly intractable problems into Her loving hands.

The Queen wields the power of the King over the entire universe. She travels the length of the vast realm in search of souls, and wherever She goes, She claims Her dominion.

WEEPING OVER THE WORLD

Looking very sad. Our Lady said, "Do not offend
the Lord our God anymore, because He is already much offended."
~ *The last words of Our Lady of Fatima to the seers,*
October 13th, 1917.[84]

Fatima reminds us that wars and cataclysms are punishment
for our sin…. Fatima is an alarm signal to men to amend their lives.
It is also a loving invitation for sincere contrition, an indispensable
way to obtain pardon of God our Father.
~ *Fr. Antonio Martins, S.J., translator of*
Sr. Lucia's Memoirs.[85]

"Father, you told me to let you know if the Pilgrim Virgin Statue would weep. Well, it is weeping now – come immediately!"[86]

The urgent message was from Fr. Joseph Breault, the Custodian of the Pilgrim Virgin Statue in 1972, who placed the call to Fr. Elmo Romagossa on the evening of July 17th that year. Fr. Romagossa happened to be the editor of the local Catholic diocesan newspaper, and he immediately rushed to the New Orleans church where the Pilgrim Virgin was being displayed and captured a number of vivid photographic images of tears flowing down the face of a Statue sculpted out of the hard wood of a Brazilian cedar tree. It was

84 Haffert, *Her Own Words*, 259.

85 Johnston, *Great Sign*, 5

86 Dialogue slightly adapted from the article, "The Tears of Our Lady Wet My Finger," by Fr. Elmo Romagosa, Executive Editor of the *Clarion Herald*, New Orleans, 7/20/72. All subsequent references to the weeping statue in New Orleans are from this same primary source unless otherwise noted.

neither the first nor last time that the Statue was seen to weep.

How in the world can we explain this phenomenon except as a continuance of the message of Fatima exhorting people to turn away from their sins and to stop offending God?

When Dr. Plinio Corrêa de Oliveira happened to see the photographs of the weeping Statue in the *Folha de Sâo Paulo*, the leading newspaper in the capital city of Brazil, he had the same thought that any sane observer of the phenomenon would have had: Our Lady is still trying to wake the world up to the enormity of its sins and offenses against God. "These mysterious tears," wrote Dr. Plinio, "show Our Lady of Fatima crying over the modern world, as Our Lord once cried over Jerusalem. Tears of most tender affection, tears of deep pain for the punishment that will come." Then he added prophetically: "It will come to the men of the twentieth century, if they do not reject immorality and corruption.... Reader, there is still time, therefore, to stop the punishment!"[87] Dr. Plinio would have been pleased to know that he was not alone in that assessment. As great an authority on the modern age as Pope John Paul II himself said, "If the statue of Our Lady weeps, she has reason to weep."[88]

"Immorality," "corruption," "punishment," "weeping for sin" are foreign terms to a generation that has become inured to sin and its consequences. Apathy toward sin is perhaps a greater danger than sin itself because it hardens us to the terrible consequences of sin. Thankfully the Queen of Heaven does not share this common human spiritual malaise. Rather, She brings the antidote to sin and apathy: tears.

Her weeping is meant to touch our hearts by a tangible display of Her suffering. Who can be apathetic toward the tears of a Mother? Yet, the tears are not for Her. They are for us, to remind us of our need to wake up to the true crisis of our times, which is a spiritual one. This, indeed, is Our Lady's way: the urgent call to conversion through an appeal from a Mother's heart. And when we see the exponential increase in the amount of sinfulness in our age, it is evident that Her message is more urgent than ever because time is running out.

87   Plinio Corrêa de Oliveira, "Tears, a Miraculous Warning," *Folha de Sau Paulo*, 08/06/72.

88   Kaczmarek, *Wonders She Performs*, 164.

JACINTA'S CONCERN FOR THE LOSS OF SOULS

In her *Memoirs*, Sr. Lucia recalled the extraordinary penances for sinners that little Jacinta performed during the rest of her short life after the apparitions. Jacinta was privileged with numerous private visions of Our Lady after the public apparitions, particularly during her period of convalescence in the Lisbon hospital.[89] In these visions Our Lady apparently revealed to Jacinta that "sins of the flesh" and "sins of impurity" were those sins by which the greatest number of souls were lost.[90] Thereafter, Jacinta was profoundly concerned about people who offended God in this way. This extraordinary concern came from a girl who had not even reached adolescence. We may ask whether she in her innocence even understood the nature and implications of these terms. Full human awareness or not, Lucia described Jacinta's ongoing revulsion at the thought that souls could end up in Hell:

> The vision of hell filled [Jacinta] with horror to such a degree that every penance and mortification was as nothing in her eyes if it could only prevent souls from going there.... Jacinta often sat thoughtfully on the ground or on a rock, and exclaimed:
> "Oh! Hell! Hell! How sorry I am for the souls who go to hell! And the people down there, burning alive, like wood in the fire!"
> Then, shuddering, she knelt down with her hands joined and recited the prayer that Our Lady had taught us: '*O my Jesus! Forgive us our sins, save us from the fires of hell. Lead all souls to Heaven, especially those most in need.*'[91]

Lucia believed that Jacinta was endowed with a special grace of concern for souls.

---

89   Apostoli, Fatima for Today, 145; cf. also Haffert, *Her Own Words*, chs. 3-4, for a fuller account of Jacinta's sufferings.

90   John M. Haffert, *Deadline: The Third Secret of Fatima* (Asbury: The 101 Foundation, Inc., 2001), 281, 222.

91   Haffert, *Her Own Words*, 164.

Perhaps a hundred years ago a message detailing the outrageous sins of the century's end – partial birth abortion and euthanasia, wide-scale promiscuity, pornography and homosexual activism, the demands for so-called gay marriage, etc. – would have been so foreign to the average person's understanding that Our Lady could not announce those specific sins to the world as such. Her message would have been utterly incomprehensible. But She foresaw these same sins with Her eternal vision and She understood their deadly effects on souls. The Angel of Portugal used terms such as "outrages, sacrileges and indifference by which [God] is offended," and Our Lady in turn asked the children to offer themselves and their sufferings "for the sins by which He is offended and in supplication for the conversion of sinners."

In light of that saintly child of Fatima,[92] we must each ask ourselves how we would rate our own penances for sinners and our own desire to save souls. How would we rate our concern for a world awash in immorality and corruption?

THE SINFULNESS OF THE MODERN WORLD

Fatima's relevance to the 21st Century world is displayed before our eyes literally every day as we see the drama of unrepentant sin played out in our public lives and private associations. Today we see more clearly than ever before what Our Lady meant about *the power of sin* to drag souls to Hell.

Were we to focus on the "sins of the flesh" alone, we would see perhaps a glimpse of the horrors that Jacinta witnessed when the chasm of Hell opened up before her eyes on that July day in 1917. Sins of impurity are now a business. One hundred years after the apparitions, there is now an entire industry of pornography that is exponentially more extensive, cruel, destructive, and diabolical than anyone in the First World War era could have possibly imagined. Shockingly, revenues generated by the global porn industry are $97 *billion* with the United States alone responsible for $10-$12 billion

---

92   Jacinta and her brother, Francisco, were officially beatified by Pope John Paul II on May 13th, 2000 and canonized by Pope Francis on May 13th, 2017

of that.[93] According to the economic database of the International Monetary Fund, worldwide pornography revenues surpass the GDPs of the poorest 126 nations of the world.[94] Do we wonder why Our Lady weeps?

The vision of Hell that God chose to show to the children through Our Lady's hands was an act of supreme mercy. God, in His Mercy, wants to save our souls from eternal death, and Our Lady is the effective envoy of that message. If such a message was not fully comprehensible a century ago, it should be much clearer now.

A NEW KIND OF PROPHETIC CALL

But certainly conversion is difficult. Human beings are attached to sin. Our hearts are often hard and our attitudes resistant to the transforming effect of God's grace. That is why Our Lady's way is not the way of denunciation, which would serve to alienate sinners from God's mercy when they need it most. Our Lady's unique motherly grace wins conversions by opening doors and softening hearts to the message of Jesus' Gospel. Touching hearts is the first step to leading souls along the path of conversion. If a biblical prophet *drives* souls to God with righteous scolding and condemnations, God's Mother leads them back to Him by the sheer force of Her beauty and love.

The immediate past Custodian of the Pilgrim Virgin Statue, Carl Malburg, notes that, even though miracles happen everywhere the Statue travels, Our Lady is not attempting to dazzle people into believing in God. In fact, Malburg tended to downplay the miraculous happenings that often surround the Statue's visits because he felt they could distract from the real message of Fatima.[95] When I asked Mr. Malburg if there was any particular grace or way that Our Lady touches people most deeply, he responded candidly, "The most important [ways she touches people] are spiritual things, certainly. High on that list is a peaceful spirit. People come with heavy problems and burdens and after praying before this special Image, they seem to be

93 Chris Morris, "Things Are Looking Up in America's Porn Industry," CNBC, 01/20/15; http://www.nbcnews.com/business/business-news/things-are-looking-americas-porn-industry-n289431.

94 "World Economic Outlook Database," International Monetary Fund, April 2016.

95 Rex W. Huppke, "Statue and its caretaker make journeys of faith," *Chicago Tribune*, 3/25/04.

able to regain a spirit of peace and resignation to their crosses."[96]

Our Lady's mission, through means of the Pilgrim Virgin Statue, is to bring people to conversion and to usher in a new era of peace for the world. She seems to make the world a more peaceful place by touching one heart at a time. She is the perfect missionary of Her Son's transforming personal invitation to conversion: "I have not come to call the righteous," He said, "but sinners" (Mt 9:13). John Haffert believed that the message of Fatima and the work of salvation is always most effective when done "person-to-person",[97] and I believe him.

CONVERSION IS THE CORE MESSAGE OF FATIMA

In the Statue's inaugural travels throughout North America (late Forties-early Fifties), Msgr. William C. McGrath, the Statue's first Custodian, expressed his ongoing admiration for Our Lady's ability to change hearts through Her ineffable presence in the Pilgrim Virgin Statue:

> The countless unceasing miracles of grace, whereby sinners have returned to the sacraments in almost every one of the nine hundred parishes visited, are evidence of the fact that the Blessed Mother is calling her own children back to the wounded Heart of her Divine Son, in preparation of whatever may lie ahead in the uncertain days before us. In their thousands, to the amazement of priests from end to end of America, they have returned to the sacraments after having been out of the Church from five to fifty years. Repeatedly we have been told that nothing like this has ever been seen before and it is idle to seek for any merely human explanation.[98]

As someone who has accompanied the Pilgrim Virgin Statue to various places around the world and in America, I can categorically affirm Msgr.

96   Thomas J. McKenna, personal interview with Carl Malburg, 11/30/02.

97   Haffert, *Shake the World*, 170.

98   Msgr. William C. McGrath, *Fatima or World Suicide?* (Ontario: The Scarboro Foreign Mission Society, 1951), 19.

McGrath's insight. Every place the Statue goes the priests are overwhelmed by the number of confessions they are called upon to hear. The vast majority of people who see Her are utterly captivated by Her beauty and wish to change their lives to conform to a higher standard. In 1985 the auxiliary bishop of the Archdiocese of Omaha, Bishop Anthony Milone, noted that "the statue's beauty is enough to melt the heart of a very hard person."[99] How true!

Monsignor was also aware that the Statue could have an enormous impact on those who did not share the Catholic or even the Christian faith. For example, in one parish in Lake Charles, Louisiana there were ten converts taking instructions, all attributed to the visit of the Pilgrim Virgin in March of 1948. Some in the Deep South, of course, accused Catholics of worshipping a statue, but the Monsignor noted that an overwhelming number of Protestants were extremely favorable toward the Statue and even found a renewed respect for Catholics on account of the Statue's visit. And sometimes the respect was shown in unexpected ways. "At one hospital," he said, "a Jewish doctor…stood in silent prayer and respect for several minutes in front of the statue. As he later explained to the sisters, 'It just does something to you.'" These incidents are only a small sampling of many more that could be cited, but it shows the very genuine desire on the part of many non-Catholics to learn about the message of Fatima and its effect on their lives.[100]

Something in this Statue exerts a special attraction upon souls. It is not something physical or sensible; it is more like Our Lady speaks to each one through the expression of the Statue's features. The Statue's presence is always an occasion for unique graces. On a 1976 trip to Latin America, for example, an avowed atheist crossed the Statue's path at the Bucaramanga airport in Colombia, and began to weep copiously. It took only *one glance* at the Statue for this man to break down. In Merida, Venezuela, a sinner who had stayed away from the Sacraments for more than forty years approached the Statue and, after looking into Her very expressive eyes, said, "Her gaze has converted me. I'm going to confession."[101] This pattern of heartfelt repentance because of a visit of Our Lady is truly remarkable.

99   Kaczmarek, *Wonders She Performs*, 149; citing the bishop's 10/6/85 interview in the *World-Herald* newspaper of Omaha, Nebraska.

100   Msgr. William C. McGrath, "Our Lady of Fatima, the Pilgrim Virgin, continues her American tour," *Scarboro Foreign Mission* Magazine (July-August 1949), 49.

101   Report of Luis Guillermo, 2013.

One priest in the Upper Peninsula of Michigan once said that he had seen more returns to the Church, more confessions, more frequenting of the sacraments and more *charity* in his parish when the Pilgrim Virgin Statue visited than at any other time in his priesthood.[102] He is one of many priests who have said the same.

A REMARKABLE SCENE IN AN AIRPORT

Our Lady repeatedly asks us to turn away from our sins and to stop offending Jesus, but we must recall that it is not just the many "outrages and sacrileges" of our generation that offend Him. It is also our *indifference* to the divine love that He holds out to all. Our Lady leads souls out of apathy and indifference to conversion of heart, a rebirth of religious fervor, and to the tangible change of life that accompanies Her message. There is something about Her radiance that is like an open air passage to the soul fanning into flame the smoldering embers of faith that linger faintly in the hearts of those who have lost their spiritual fervor. No flame of faith, however slight, is lost on Our Lady.

In 2004 I was given the task of picking up the Pilgrim Virgin Statue in Chicago and taking it to Brazil on pilgrimage. When I arrived at O'Hare International Airport with the Statue and approached the security check point, one of the agents asked in a kind and lighthearted way what was in the bag. When I responded that it was a Statue of the Blessed Mother he got a startled look on his face and became serious and focused, as did the other three agents who had overheard the conversation. They were all very attentive. One of the security agents asked, almost in astonishment, whether this was the Statue that he had seen in the newspaper a few days before, and one of the other agents drew closer to hear my response. When I replied that indeed it was the uniquely special International Pilgrim Virgin Statue, they all looked at each other and got very excited. They could not believe it. They began asking questions about the Statue and asked if they could see it up close.

The security agents became very concerned that the Statue would go through the X-ray machine safely. I explained that we do it all the time with

102   Kaczmarek, *Wonders She Performs*, 88, citing the testimony of Rev. E. Brodeur of St. Stanislaus Kostka Parish, Marquette, Michigan, U.P.

care. But that wasn't good enough for them. One of the agents held the head of Our Lady as it went into the machine while another reached in at the other end to lift the Statue so it wouldn't roll on the belt. I shouldn't have been surprised at their interest, but I marveled at how easily Our Lady's image becomes embedded in the hearts and minds of the faithful when they see Her in any medium. They were very intrigued with the beauty of the Statue and with Her mission, so I offered them pictures of Her which they graciously accepted, even asking for extras for other agents who were not on duty that day. Without much delay, I passed through the inspection area and proceeded to my gate. As I settled in to wait for my flight, I found a place in the back waiting area of our gate, unzipped the top part of the padded carrying case so that I could see Her and began to pray the Rosary.

Sometime later there was a commotion near the gate as a woman came running into the seating area and anxiously scanned all the seats. I had looked up when she arrived so our eyes met, and that was when she saw the Statue and made a beeline for us. "I found you! I found you!" she kept repeating with sobs of joy. She must have been in her mid-thirties and was dressed in a business suit, but despite her prim and proper appearance, she was out of breath and oblivious to the looks she was getting from others. Obviously she had been hurrying from elsewhere and simply cast all decorum aside as she knelt before the Statue with tears coming from her eyes repeating, "I found you!" This was a very touching display of devotion, which one doesn't see often, much less in an airport terminal. When she finally got over her initial emotion, she told me what led her to my departure gate. Apparently, just a few moments after I had gone through the security area, the woman went through the same line and asked the airport security agents what the commotion was that she had observed from the back of the line. The men casually mentioned that my precious cargo was that famous Fatima statue that travels the world and had appeared on the front page of the *Chicago Tribune* a few days before.

"Our Lady of Fatima!" she exclaimed to the agents. The very hearing of the name seemed to ignite a bonfire under her.

"Do you know what gate that man went to?" she asked urgently; but they didn't know.

This caused her to rush through security and to make the rounds of every gate in the terminal for close to forty-five minutes until she finally, breathlessly, discovered us at the last gate and made a beeline to the Statue. I finally understood why she could only sob, "I found you! I found you!" Her sentiment was very moving and helped me to see how easy it is for Our Lady to touch hearts and to awaken in them the desire for God. All Our Lady needs is a person's willingness to respond to grace, and apparently this young woman had that willingness in abundance.

The story had a backdrop. "I'm a business executive," she said to me. "I've been away from the Church for so long, and I've deeply regretted it, but I've just not had the time…. No," she corrected herself, "I've just not *made* the time to go. So many other things have always gotten in the way. My mother has always been telling me about the Blessed Mother and asking me to pray to Her, but I've kind of ignored Her."

"Then," she continued, "when the men at security told me that *She* was here, I knew there was a special reason why we crossed paths, and I just *had* to find Her. That's why I've been running through this airport trying to find you! I just have to come back to Church. My mother's been urging me. This is a *clear* sign."

Still somewhat breathless when she told the story, she began to calm down and stare with intense admiration at the Statue's beauty and with good reason. She was another soul that had been attracted by the Blessed Mother's net of love. In fact, she was so taken up by the grace of the moment that she threw human respect out the window and sat on the ground before the Pilgrim Virgin as if there was no one else in the entire airport. There were, in fact, many dozens of people walking by and many people in the gate area, but she didn't see any of them. I wondered if she even saw me. She only focused on the Statue and all Her beauty.

"I have to come back," she now repeated out loud. "This is a sign."

A few moments later, the woman snapped out of her reverie and said, "Oh, I've gotta go get my boss. He has to see Her." Whereupon the woman darted off to another gate and dragged a rather beleaguered-looking man in a suit over to see the Statue and told him the story of her significant discovery just a quarter of an hour earlier. But just to prove that grace operates uniquely in different lives, it appeared that the man was almost completely unaffected by the Statue, but he nodded and showed all the appropriate interest that he could muster for the sake of his colleague. His lack of matching enthusiasm, however, did not stop this zealous woman from singing Our Lady's praises with the greatest eloquence and devotion.

My airport terminal experience with this young lady was a truly vivid and moving scene, and one that I will never forget. It's the kind of story that makes all the sacrifices of international travel with the Pilgrim Virgin Statue seem like minor inconveniences when compared to the graces that Our Lady lavishes on souls. It reminded me that God truly owns the human soul. He creates within each soul a space reserved just for Him, a conscience, an inner life; and Our Lady knows when a soul needs a spark of divine life to set it aflame when the time is right. This woman only needed to *hear* that Our Lady's Statue was in the airport, and she was inspired. She was smitten by the aura of love that Our Lady conveys through the Statue. The more I reflect on what our Lady accomplishes in souls through that power of attraction, the more I see it as a greater miracle than what She accomplished through the Miracle of the Sun.

I pulled out of my bag a holy card of the Pilgrim Virgin Statue, which I touched to the image and handed to the renewed young woman for safe-keeping. "I'll cherish this forever!" she said as she ran to catch a plane that she gladly would have missed had her boss not been there.

A HEALER OF SOULS

*My Immaculate Heart will be your comfort and the way
which will lead you to God.*
~*Our Lady of Fatima, Second Apparition, June 13th, 1917.*

From the very onset of the Public Ministry of Jesus, Our Lady has been obtaining miracles for people from the hands of Her divine Son. The miracle that Jesus wrought at the Wedding at Cana (Jn 2:1-12) was obtained through Our Lady's request: She saw the need of the couple and brought the need to Him who is the Source of all grace and favor. The effect was spectacular – dozens of gallons of water were transformed into the finest wine – but the effect went far beyond the simple fact that Our Lady's intervention saved a newly-wed couple from embarrassment at their wedding. The theological truth of this story is simple and at the same time quite profound: Our Lady draws down the power of Christ from Heaven on the real needs of people who ask Her intercession. Miracles, healings, conversions, and inner transformations are all signs of the grace of God entering the world. They are all signs of Christ's Kingdom.

Are we to believe that Our Lady's special intercessory power ceased after the Wedding at Cana? Hardly! As the Mother of Christ, She became Mother of the Church after the Resurrection and, in a very real way, the *Mother of all humanity* when She was assumed into Heaven and glorified. It is this Heavenly Lady, with enormous privileges as Queen and special powers of intercession, who appeared at Fatima and exercises Her maternal love for humanity everywhere She goes.

In fact, some believe that Her appearance at Fatima on May 13th, 1917 itself was a response to an act of intercession made at the highest level of the Church. Pope Benedict XV, who reigned as Roman Pontiff during the First World War, initiated a worldwide novena on May 5th, 1917 to pray for the needs of suffering humanity and for an end to the First World War. The Novena culminated on the ninth day of prayer, May 13th.[103] The Queen of Peace *heard* the prayer from the Holy Father's heart. And the apparitions at Fatima were Our Lady's response.

THE POWER OF INTERCESSION

Devout little Lucia, as a ten-year-old child, was intimately aware of the power of Our Lady's intercession on behalf of poor sinners. We will remember that, from the beginning of the apparitions, Lucia was asking about the afterlife status of some of her friends and also about whether Our Lady would take the three children to heaven. (Lucia was a shrewd negotiator, even at a young age.) In the second apparition Lucia asked for the cure of a crippled boy. In subsequent apparitions she presented the needs of numerous other souls to Our Lady who generally responded that most of the requests would be granted *if people amend their lives.* Our Lady's concern for the physical wellbeing of bodies, while very real, is always tied to Her deepest concern for the eternal welfare of souls. I suspect She may have been present at the encounter in the Temple when Jesus sought out the crippled man He had just healed and appealed to him: "Do not sin anymore, so that nothing worse may happen to you" (Jn 5:14). Heaven's concern for the material is surpassed by its zeal for the spiritual.

We also see here the cascading effect of the power of personal intercession. Our Lord Jesus Christ interceded for sinful humanity and opened the gates of Heaven to us by His sacrificial offering to the Father. Our Lady brings to Her Son the needs of the poor and sinful human race. Lucia brings the specific needs of our loved ones to God personally and, I might add, most effectively with the help of Our Lady.

---

103 Kaczmarek, *Wonders She Performs*, 66. In this we are reminded of the prayer of another holy bishop, Bp. Juan de Zummáraga of Mexico, whose intercession for his people, it is believed, brought about the wondrous appearances of Our Lady of Guadalupe in 1531.

HEALINGS FLOW OUT OF FATIMA

In her *Memoirs*, Sr. Lucia recalls the time when her own mother fell seriously ill and was at the point of death. Lucia's sisters actually blamed her for their mother's illness and taunted her to pray to the Lady for a cure. Lucia offered that humiliation to God and prayed a novena to Our Lady of Fatima for the cure of her mother. Lucia ran to the apparition site at the Cova da Iria to make her prayer:

> At the Cova I placed my request before Our Lady and unburdened myself of all my sorrow, shedding copious tears. Then I went home comforted by the hope that my beloved Mother in Heaven would hear my prayer and restore health to my mother on earth. When I reached home my mother was already feeling somewhat better. Three days later she was able to resume her work around the house.[104]

Likewise, many miracles of healing have occurred at the very place where Our Lady appeared. In 1946 Mr. John Haffert witnessed a miracle at the Sanctuary of Fatima when a young woman was instantaneously cured of a brain tumor; he was present for another extraordinary healing the following year at the same place.[105] The second Bishop of Leiria-Fatima, Most Rev. John Venancio, experienced Fatima's healing power in a unique way even before he became a bishop. During a visit to his sister's home, he discovered that her husband had been suffering from chronic and sharp sciatica pain for years. In the course of their conversation, the future bishop spoke of Sr. Lucia to his brother-in-law, and the man blurted out: "Oh! If she really saw the Blessed Virgin, she could cure me!" (It is unclear whether the man was referring to the Virgin Herself or to Sr. Lucia.) However, at that very instant, the chronic pain left him and never returned.[106]

These few stories – among many possible healing stories that have taken place in or near the sanctuary itself – are but a preface to the worldwide ministry of healing that Our Lady carries out wherever the International Pilgrim

104   Haffert, *Her Own Words*, 128-29.

105   Haffert, *Russia Converted*, 78-98.

106   Haffert, *Her Own Words*, 181-82.

Virgin Statue goes. We might say that the apparitions of 1917 opened up a font of healing grace at a distinct place and time in history, a stream that Our Lady directs to those who need it at *any place and any time.* The history of healings in the presence or in the wake of the Statue will testify to this truth.

CURE OF A DYING PREGNANT WOMAN

When the International Pilgrim Virgin Statue entered the United States on December 8th, 1947 something miraculous occurred, perhaps as a testimony to the enormous grace being poured out upon our country at that time. After its month-long inaugural tour, the Statue left Canada and entered the U.S. through Niagara Falls. Niagara Falls was a truly symbolic entry point for the Statue to come to America. Few know that the Niagara Falls were consecrated to Our Lady Queen of Peace in 1861 by Bishop Lynch of Toronto as an appeal to ending the American Civil War.[107] When the Pilgrim Virgin Statue entered the City of Buffalo She was received by Most Rev. John O'Hara, then-Bishop of Buffalo, and brought to the Cathedral of St. Joseph. It was reported that about one-third of the population of Buffalo, some two hundred thousand people, came to see Her and caused the largest traffic jam in the city's history.[108]

Mr. Joseph Desjardins, a Buffalo resident, heard of the Statue's arrival and interpreted it as Our Lady's personal desire to help him in his need. Actually, the one who was in need was Desjardin's wife who was pregnant with their third child. The month before, she had slipped and fallen on the ice and was rushed to the Sisters of Charity Hospital where she had remained in critical condition for the better part of a month. To make matters worse, she lost the baby in the fall and then developed peritonitis, which was a fatal disease in those days. Her condition deteriorated day-to-day. By December 8th, the day of the Statue's arrival, Mr. Desjardins was desperate to see the Pilgrim Virgin Statue and beg for help. In a sworn statement,[109] he later described his approach to the Statue in these terms:

107   "Our Lady of Fatima Comes to America," *The Scapular* Magazine, November-December 1947.

108   Haffert, *Russia Converted*, 211.

109   From the notarized statement of Mr. Joseph (Bill) Desjardin, dated 3/30/89.

Upon learning of the statue's coming, I knew that I had to be there; that my Mother had come to help me. So I asked a friend to take my place at work and I began walking, sometimes running, through the crowded streets toward the cathedral which was about two miles away.

I arrived at the entrance of the already jammed cathedral just as the statue of Our Lady of Fatima was being carried up the steps. I forced myself through the crowd and found a vantage point in the middle aisle from where I would get a good look. The whole time I was praying and pleading...

Suddenly it happened! It seemed as if it were just the two of us. Our Lady and me. I looked at her and she looked at me... and smiled. I had a feeling at that moment, a feeling of certainty that my dying wife had been healed. A feeling of new life and exaltation came over my body and soul.

He then described his euphoria as he ran back to the hospital: "I am not sure if I walked or ran all the way to the hospital. It was like floating on air and it seemed to arrive in no time at all," he said. When he arrived, out of breath, at his wife's hospital room he was greeted by a rather overbearing nun who announced to him that he had to stay out of the room and let his wife rest because she was dying! Yet, there was a commotion in the room that signaled something extraordinary had just taken place. As it happened, Mr. Desjardins' wife had been *instantaneously and totally cured a short time earlier* and was sitting on the edge of her bed dangling her feet, full of joy: "I just had a miracle!" she told everyone. The nun didn't want to believe that she had been cured and did not want to let her leave the hospital, but both husband and wife insisted that she leave for home right then. Mrs. Desjardins felt so full of life and joy that she even refused a wheelchair to take her out of the hospital.

The family doctor, hearing of the miracle, asked to see Mrs. Desjardins the next day to confirm that there were no lingering problems. He attested to a complete and total healing but also announced that she would never be able to have any more children due to the extent of the complications she had suffered in the original fall. Perhaps the greatest miracle was that neither the hospital nor the doctor would accept a single cent for their services.

In January of 2010 I contacted the eldest of the Desjardins children, Mrs. Anne Fox, who confirmed her mother's severe fall and her miraculous recovery back in 1947. Medical records kept by the family showed that the mother had the accident and a stillborn birth on November 10th, 1947, which also confirmed that she spent nearly a month in the hospital before the miracle. Mrs. Fox also verified that, in spite of the doctor's pessimism about future childbearing, her mother had borne two more children, one of whom was a son and the biggest child in the family.

TWO HUMBLE HEALINGS

We could extend this chapter with many long and extraordinary accounts of miraculous healings at the hands of Our Lady, but I believe a couple of summary stories about other credible healings associated with the Statue will be enough to affirm our basic point about Our Lady's incredible powers of healing.

In the Statue's inaugural year touring the United States, a priest who had been hit in the eye by a baseball bat as a child, reported that he had been cured of blindness (in June of 1948) after praying before the Statue in Oklahoma City. A physician told him the healed eye was perfect. In August of the same year, a Benedictine nun who attended the famous Fatima Week of prayer St. Meinrad, Indiana (see Chapter 10) asked Our Lady to heal her from a chronic infection on her lip that had afflicted the nun for twenty-one years and that no doctor could treat successfully. She prayed for the cure during the Statue's visit and was completely healed.[110]

We thus end this chapter as we began, repeating the profound truth about Our Lady's intercession: Our Lady draws down the power of Christ from Heaven on the real needs of people who ask Her intercession. Miracles, healings, conversions, and inner transformations are all signs of the grace of God entering the world, all signs of Christ's Kingdom. As with Our Lord's miracles during His Public Ministry in Palestine two thousand years ago, the healings of Our Lady are signs that direct our eyes to the more important reason for our earthly life; that is, *to save our souls.* Spiritual healing through physical healings and conversions is the reason that wonders abound wherever the International Pilgrim Virgin Statue goes.

---

110   Both stories in this section come from a contemporary source: Lillian Kellard, "New York Listens," *The Scapular* Magazine, March-April, 1949.

This is the first statue of Our Lady of Fatima, sculpted in 1941, by Guilherme Ferreira Thedim, the older brother of Jose Ferreira Thedim who sculpted the International Pilgrim Virgin Statue.

In December 1946 Jose Thedim's original statue went on pilgrimage to Lisbon for the feast of the Immaculate Conception. At one point during the procession four white doves were released into the air and three of them settled on the feet of Our Lady's Statue and remained there for the rest of the two week trip without eating or drinking.

Bishop Jose da Silva, first bishop of Fatima, blessing the Pilgrim Virgin before it traveled to the United States. Holding the crown at right is Mrs. John Wiley whose husband was the U.S. Ambassador to Portugal.

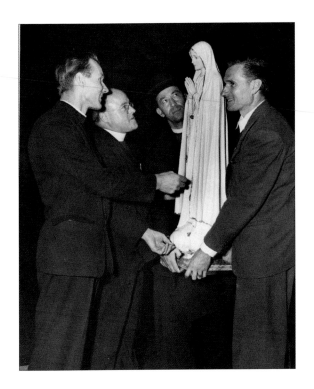

Religious Peace Mission

A statue of Our Lady of Fatima, being used in a spiritual effect to re Christianize Russia, is shown after it was carried from the Pan American World Airways Clipper Flying Mist on which it arrived in New York today (Oct. 17) from Lisbon. John Haffert (right), well known Catholic writer and lecturer, and the Very Rev. Jose D'Oliveira, secretary to the bishop of Fatima, Portugal, brought the statue on the Lisbon-New York leg of its pilgrimage. Welcoming them are the Rev. George O'Mara (left), of St. Boniface's, Sea Cliff, N.Y., and the Rev. Patrick Moore of Scaroboro Bluffs, Ontario, Canada. The statue, made of delicately carved wood, immediately started out on a tour of Roman Catholic dioceses in Canada and through the United States and around the world, carrying through a 30 year old prophecy that such an act would bring permanent peace to the world. Haffert, son of Mayor William A. Haffert of Sea Isle City, N.J., said he would go along on part of the U. S. portion of the tour.

From Pan American World Airways
La Guardia Field, N. Y.

The first day of the Pilgrimage, on the grounds of Ottawa University, Ottawa, Canada. Facing the camera is His Excellency Archbishop Vachon. Immediately in front of the Archbishop is Mr. John Haffert, who brought the statue by plane from Fatima. Holding [the] statue is Father Timothy O'Sullivan, CSSR, who assisted in the 50 day Canadian tour. Extreme left, near statue, Canon Galamba de Oliveira, of Fatima.

Children of St. Michael's Church, Biloxi, bid goodbye to Pilgrim Virgin statue as it leaves for Lafayette, Louisiana.

(From the Daily News, August 26, 1948, Chicago)

The Statue of Our Lady of Fatima is carried in solemn procession from the parish convent chapel to St. Clara Roman Catholic Church, 6400 Woodlawn Ave., on Wednesday night. Two thousand persons greeted the famous statue.

The Pilgrim Virgin being venerated by faithful in Baltimore 1949.

OUR LADY OF FATIMA

THE PILGRIM VIRGIN STATUE
will be at
HOLY CROSS CHURCH
329 West 42nd Street, New York 18, N. Y.
Wed., Thurs. and Fri., April 4th, 5th and 6th, 1951
Statue may be visited all day
Special Services every day at 12:10, 5:30 and 8:1

Holy Card

THE PILGRIM VIRGIN STATUE

America's "pilgrim Virgin" is one of two images of Our Lady of Fatima blessed for similar pilgrimages by the Bishop of Fatima in 1947 at the famous Portuguese shrine. Both are hand-carved from cedarwood by Thedim, famed Portuguese sculptor, who designed the original now in the Fatima basilica. The first statue was blessed on May 13, 1947, and is now touring Europe; the second on October 13, 1947, anniversary of Our Lady's final apparition at Fatima, in the presence of 200,000 pilgrims. Immediately after the blessing America's Pilgrim Virgin was flown to the United States and taken by automobile to Ottawa, Canada. There it was crowned by the Archbishop, Most Reverend Alexandre Vachon, D.D., preparatory to starting its long journey through Canada and the United States. During the first year of its tour in this country, the famed image visited 32 Dioceses in 20 different States, and was venerated by more than 5,000,000 people.

The purpose of this pilgrimage is to invite millions of people to join in a Crusade of prayer and reparation for world peace and the conversion of Russia, as promised by Our Blessed Mother at Fatima in 1917. The pilgrimage is under the direction of Most Reverend John F. O'Hara, D.D., C.S.C., Bishop of Buffalo.

(OVER)

Fr. Desmond Stringer, Fr. Alphonsus Chafe, and Msgr. McGrath (all Scarboro Foreign Mission) with Pope Pius XII and Pilgrim Virgin Statue of Our Lady of Fatima.

This picture was taken in June 1970 at Our Lady of the Assumption Catholic Church in Albuquerque, New Mexico. Photos taken by Thomas Collard, a lifelong devotee of Our Lady.

The Pilgrim Virgin clothed in the Carmelite Habit as she appeared to the three children in the last Fatima apparition in October 1917. Photo 1970's.

Pilgrim Virgin in San Francisco in the 1970's.

Photograph taken of the Pilgrim Virgin Statue weeping while on tour in New Orleans, Louisiana July 17, 1972. This photograph was circulated by the Associated Press and was published in newspapers around the world.

These photos were published by The Baltimore Sun newspapers in April 1973.

A nun touches her rosary to the statue.

Spectators watch as the statue is transported across the Baltimore harbor on a Baltimore City fire boat.

Pilgrim Virgin in South Vietnam February 1974. Some 2,000,000 South Vietnamese turned out to greet the statue and persons of all faiths met together in a union of prayer for the first time in the 4,000 year history of that country. The statue traveled throughout the country on massive floats along roads lined with thousands of people. The giant float bearing the Pilgrim Virgin statue with the Caodaist Great Temple in the background, is greeted by thousands of Caodaists in their traditional white costumes.

The Pilgrim Virgin toured Central and South America from 1975 – 1982 in the care of the Societies for the Defense of Tradition, Family and Property. Prince Bertrand of Orléans-Braganza, heir to the Brazilian Imperial throne, served as custodian occasionally. Here he is carrying the statue to the plane.

Processing to the plane.

Cardinal Bernardino Echeverría Ruiz, archbishop of Quito, Equador, traveling with the statue.

Securing the statue for the flight.

Pilgrim Virgin in a procession on a float.

Pilgrim Virgin about to begin a public procession. Professor Plinio Corrêa de Oliveira, founder of the Society for the Defense of Tradition, Family and Property, which had custodianship of the statue from 1975 to 1982, is in the foreground.
Background: Decorated van atop which the statue will be carried. Photo 1970's.

Pilgrim Virgin in long caravan procession in Sao Paulo, Brazil.

Professor Corrêa de Oliveira crowning the statue on the tarmac at Congonhas airport as she arrived in Sao Paulo, Brazil. Photo 1970's.

In October of 1992, after the fall of Communism, John Haffert made a pilgrimage to Moscow with the International Pilgrim Virgin Statue accompanied by two jumbo jets full of pilgrims (over nine hundred people), where they witnessed the reunion of the two statues that had been blessed at Fatima in October 1947. One of the 747 airplanes.

The pilgrims in Red Square.

November 7 - 9 1997 the Pilgrim Virgin Statue and John Haffert were at St. Ann Church in Erie, Pennsylvania for festivities commemorating 25 years of continued First Friday and First Saturday devotions. John Haffert being interviewed by David Blum of the Apostolate of Divine Mercy who organized the events.

Artist Dias Tavares seen here upon completion of last restoration in 1999.

Author Thomas McKenna conducting an extensive interview with John Haffert at his office in Washington, New Jersey in April 1999.

Continental Airline cabin crew on a flight from Sao Paulo, Brazil to Washington, D.C. in 2000. Upon boarding the crew moved the Pilgrim Virgin and Thomas McKenna to first class seating.

The funeral procession for John Haffert. A funeral Mass was held in the Blessed Sacrament Chapel at the National World Apostolate of Fatima Shrine of the Immaculate Heart of Mary on November 3rd, 2001. The Mass was presided over by Bishop James S. Sullivan, the National President of WAF at the time. The Pilgrim Virgin Statue was present.

Following the funeral Mass from left to right three custodians: Richard Fasanello, Thomas McKenna and Carl Malburg.

Prince Luiz of Orléans-Braganza, heir to the Imperial Throne of Brazil, crowning the Pilgrim Virgin at a conference in Vienna.

Thomas McKenna boarding a plane in Austria.

In April 2004 Thomas McKenna accompanied the Pilgrim Virgin to Austria and Italy on pilgrimage. The return trip was especially memorable as the crew was overwhelmed with the great privilege. The pilots and crew of the 747 upon arrival in Detroit.

Thomas McKenna with Captain Tom Perillo in the First Class cabin.

São Paulo, Brazil 2000 (Left to right) Thomas McKenna with the Pilgrim Virgin and Princes Luiz of Orléans-Braganza and his brother Bertrand of Orléans-Braganza, heirs to the Brazilian Imperial throne.

In October 2007 among the more than half a million people who gathered at Fatima for the 90th Anniversary of the Miracle of the Sun, was Archbishop Tadeusz Kondruchewicz, the first Catholic bishop consecrated in Russia in the post-Communist era. When he learned that the Pilgrim Virgin was present, he asked that the statue be placed on a pillar in front of the altar which is very near where Our Lady had actually appeared in 1917. Custodians Carl Malburg and Thomas McKenna look on while Archbishop Kondruchewicz prepares to crown Our Lady.

Pilgrims from Russia who accompanied the Archbishop to Fatima.

The Pilgrim Virgin visited San Diego in January of 2008. Auxiliary bishop Salvator Cordileone (later Archbishop) leading a procession with the Pilgrim Virgin from the Cathedral of St. Joseph the Worker to a park facing an abortion providing facility as an act of reparation.

In September 2009 the Pilgrim Virgin was on tour in Haiti. The statues arrival in Port-Au-Prince with custodian Carl Malburg.

Our Lady carried in procession in a church.

In May of 2014 the International Pilgrim Virgin statue went on pilgrimage to Fatima with a group of Americans. Fr. Carl Gismondi, F.S.S.P., the pilgrim's chaplain, celebrated Mass at the Capelinha in the presence of the two historic Statues, at the very spot where the Blessed Mother appeared at the Cova da Iria to the three children in 1917.

Mass celebrated in Coimbra, with the Pilgrim Virgin Statue, at the Carmelite convent where Sr. Lucia lived until she died February 13, 2005.

Bishop Constantino Luna, O.F.M leading a procession with the Pilgrim Virgin. He served as the international director of the World Apostolate of Fatima in the 1980's.

Msgr. William C. McGrath, SFM, custodian from 1947-1968.

Louis Kaczmarek served as custodian from 1983 – 1992.

(Left to right) Carl Malburg, Rose Mary Malburg, Patricia Haffert (wife of the late John Haffert), Thomas McKenna and Richard Fasanello. Photo July 2007.

Richard Fasanello on tour in Manila, Philippines. 1994.
Richard Fasanello served as custodian from 1998 – 1999.

José Ferreira Thedim – called "the Michelangelo of Portugal," sculpted the Pilgrim Virgin Statue described in this book.

Thomas McKenna with the Pilgrim Virgin in Rome, 2013.

TRANSFORMATIONS

Souls are not given as gifts; they are bought. You do not know what
they cost Jesus. Now they still have to be bought always with the same coin.
~ *St. Padre Pio, 1887-1968.*[111]

So threatening was the International Pilgrim Virgin Statue to the Communist authorities in Poland during the Cold War that the Statue was *forbidden* to exit the plane when John Haffert's 1978 Peace Flight landed at Warsaw Airport.[112] The way this incident was reported throughout that profoundly Catholic country was accurate, as long as you take into account that love for Our Lady is a vivid feature of Poland's national consciousness: *it was reported that the Russians were holding Our Lady hostage.* Her unceremonious captivity, however, would not be Our Lady's last word for Poland. She would transform that cultural and political fiasco into a resounding victory of grace.

The Russians who sequestered Our Lady's Statue at the airport posted a round-the-clock guard at the plane during the entire visit of Our Lady's peace pilgrims. Even a populace hardened to Communist atrocities was shocked by this act. When the pilgrims arrived at the famous Marian Shrine of Our Lady of Czestochowa, the Cardinal Primate of Poland, Stefan Wyszynski, told them, "You from the free world may be surprised at this, but we are not always free to do what we would like to do." That perhaps was an understatement but an accurate assessment of life under Communist rule. A

---

111   https://www.ewtn.com/padrepio/mystic/Mary.htm.
112   This entire incident and all quotes are taken from Haffert, *Dear Bishop*, 298-301.

clever priest on the flight suggested that Our Lady's image be carried symbolically throughout their visit in the form of a white-painted wire outline of the Statue. The *empty frame* idea caught on like wildfire and became a rallying cry at every stop where the pilgrims would have carried the Pilgrim Virgin Statue had they been allowed.

The Statue's imprisonment increasingly became a public relations nightmare for the Communist regime, and by the time the pilgrims left, the incident had triggered something of a fit of resentment and "a spiritual revolt", as John Haffert called it, among the faithful Poles. The Communists could oppress them, but when they began to oppress the Virgin Mother of God, the battle lines were drawn. The authorities approached Cardinal Wyszynski after the pilgrims' departure with an attitude of appeasement – something short of actual contrition – claiming that they had not meant to harm the Statue and that the whole thing was just a misunderstanding. They even wanted to appear altruistic by inviting the Statue back. In that invitation, however, they miscalculated the shrewd negotiating skills of Polish churchmen; the Cardinal and bishops took this offer as a chance to negotiate for something they had been denied for a quarter of a century: new churches.

The end result of the incident was that Cardinal Wyszynski promised to bring the Statue back the following year, and the Communist premier allowed them to build *eight new churches.*

I mentioned that the story doesn't end with Our Lady's Statue being "detained" on the tarmac at Warsaw Airport in 1978. The grace that radiated from Her symbolic captivity produced great fruit in those new churches, the first of which was christened "Queen of the World" in honor of the Peace Flight that was the effective instrument for the desired permits. That temple of God was the first church built in Catholic Poland in twenty-five years. It was consecrated the following year on August 22nd, and John Haffert triumphantly brought the Pilgrim Virgin back to Poland to hold pride of place at the ceremony. In fact, the Statue was carried into the church and placed next to the empty wire outline that symbolized Her absence throughout Poland the year before.

If the story of Our Lady's victory ended there the tale would have been extraordinary enough, but there was another negotiation behind the scenes that may have proved even more significant than the building of new churches. John Haffert describes the incident in gripping detail:

> Now on this golden day, the Feast of the Queenship of Mary, a priest
> arrived while we were at dinner after the dedication of the church, with
> the breathtaking news that shortly before the arrival of the Pilgrim Vir-
> gin statue at the new Church of Our Lady Queen of the World, official
> documents had come from the government authorizing the building of
> [a brand new] seminary!

The seminary had been Cardinal Wyszynski's dream. Anyone with a sense
of modern Church history will also know that within two months of that
first Peace Flight, a new pope named Wojtyła (Pope John Paul II) would be
elected – the first Polish pope in history.

GRACE-FILLED TRANSFORMATIONS

As the Poland story shows, nothing about Our Lady's way of operating has
the slightest hint of force or violence to it. The Mother of God is full of grace
and favor. She is both the humble woman of the Gospel and the radiant
Queen of the Apocalypse, so overflowing with God's goodness that She
exercises full authority over all things in heaven and on earth. She was often
called by the Fathers of the Church the *New Eve* because of Her preeminent
role in the salvation of the human race.

When the Pilgrim Virgin Statue travels around the world, it conveys a
sense of the "moral presence" of the Blessed Mother with it. This was a term
coined by John Haffert and regularly used by the current Custodian of the
Statue, Mr. Patrick Sabat, when he speaks to audiences about the long-stand-
ing Catholic tradition of venerating statues. Our Lady does not want anyone
to worship Her. She wants all to worship God. The great Marian apostle, St.
Louis de Montfort, once captured this truth in a simple but clear example
when he said that "it would be easier to separate the light from the sun" than
to separate Mary from Jesus.[113]

113   St. Louis Marie de Montfort, Trans. Fr. Frederick Faber, *True Devotion to Mary* (Rockford: TAN
Books and Publishers, Inc., 1985), 39.

Her vocation as mother of Jesus was to bring Christ to the world; Her vocation as Mother of the Church is to bring the world back to Christ. These two callings of Our Lady foreshadow the vocation and mission of the Church throughout history. That is the very reason She has appeared in history with the transformational powers of God's greatest believer. Nowhere is that power more evident than in the International Pilgrim Virgin Statue of Our Lady of Fatima.

REVOLUTIONS, RESURRECTIONS, AND RECONCILIATIONS

When we speak of transformations we are talking about the action of grace influencing the real circumstances of human life, the cumulative force of which brings powerful, peaceful change. The 1978-79 Poland scenario is one such transformation, but it is one of many. These transformations take place in various ways, some of which can be thought of as revolutions, resurrections, and reconciliations.

Perhaps the most immediate of all Fatima transformations took place in an unforeseen way in Portugal itself soon after the apparitions. The political strongman who ruled Portugal after the Communist take-over in 1910, Alfonso Costa, boasted that he would eliminate all religious practice in that country in two generations.[114] But the joke was on him. In the space of nine years his own government was overthrown and a representative government with a Catholic leader was eventually installed. It was a revolution of grace that undermined the Communist plan to capture a foothold for its global revolution in Spain and Portugal. The "Iberian Strategy" was Lenin's threat to make the Iberian Peninsula the starting point of the worldwide Communist revolution.[115]

Reconciliations and peace-making abound wherever the Pilgrim Virgin Statue goes. The international Peace Flights of John Haffert saw many such transformations played out on a world stage similar to what happened in Poland. The Peace Flight of December 1949, for example, brought the Pilgrim Virgin Statue to the troubled border between Pakistan and Hindu-

114   Apostoli, *Fatima for Today*, 95.
115   Haffert, *Russia Converted*, 72,102f. and Haffert, *Dear Bishop*, 163.

stan in the northwestern region of India. There had been a bloody massacre and an ongoing sectarian war between Muslims and Hindus since the partition of India in 1947 because the border was not well-defined. The day the Peace Flight arrived in the region a cease fire was declared and peace negotiations were begun. Soon after that, a peace accord was signed on the very day that the Pilgrim Virgin Statue traveled on a flower-covered train to the border of Pakistan.[116]

Both John Haffert and Louis Kaczmarek recount in their books the amazing story of the 1978 Peace Flight that made an unscheduled flight from Egypt into Israel on the Feast of the Passover that year.[117] The late-Seventies was a particularly tense time in Arab-Israeli relations, and there were no commercial airline flights passing between the two countries. While the U.S. State Department frowned on the Peace Flight as a sort of tampering in the peace process, permission for the passage was unexpectedly granted by both the Premier of Israel, Menachem Begin, and the President of Egypt, Anwar Sadat, within a twenty-four-hour period. The peace pilgrims flew from the land of Christ's exile to the land of His birth with prayer on their lips for the process of reconciliation that was just beginning between the two countries. It was the first Egypt to Israel civilian flight in history, and it was flown by an airliner bearing the bold inscription, *Queen of the World*, on its fuselage.

The Pilgrim Virgin Statute also brought about an astounding inner resurrection in the heart of a man who had been a prisoner in a Nazi concentration camp. This poor man's entire family had been killed in Auschwitz, and he saw what he called "unspeakable deeds" during his years in the camp. Afterward, the man was tormented his entire adult life by the atrocities which he had both witnessed and suffered. It was only through a visit of the Pilgrim Virgin Statue to his parish that the now-elderly man was able to find inner peace by letting go of the hatred that had consumed him for thirty-five years. He said that She "gave [him] light" and helped him banish the poison that had eaten away at his heart for so long. He had been in a prison of another sort for more than three decades, and Our Lady entered into that inner place of pain and freed him from it.[118]

116   *Soul* Magazine, January-February, 1978.

117   *Haffert, Dear Bishop, 296f.; Kaczmarek*, Wonders She Performs, 45ff.

118   Kaczmarek, *Wonders She Performs*, 86.

THE TRANSFORMATION OF HEARTS

Above all, it is clear to me that Our Lady touches hearts. That is the transformation that God desires most. Throughout my life I have had the privilege of accompanying the International Pilgrim Virgin Statue on numerous pilgrimages, both domestically and internationally, and have seen some amazing transformations take place before my very eyes. Wherever She goes She attracts attention and inspires respect; Her very presence evokes reactions of deep devotion and, at times, real changes of heart. It is especially impressive to see this when we are not in a church setting or shrines. On my July 2002 pilgrimage to Austria, I witnessed one of the most astounding examples of Our Lady's transformational power that I have ever seen.

The full-time Custodian of the Statue in 2002 was Carl Malburg. His wife Rose Mary coordinated the travels of the Pilgrim Virgin Statue for over twenty years and did an excellent job in the very complex task of arranging venues and travel plans for Our Lady's Statue around the world, some of which had to be planned more than a year in advance. Because of the miraculous aspect of this Statue and out of reverence for Her, Rose Mary would always book Her a seat on the plane for Her travels. The reader may recall that we never allow the Statue to be put in the cargo hold with the other luggage during a flight. The custom is for the Custodian to place the Statue on a purchased seat next to him in a soft padded cloth case that is well-secured for the flight. Occasionally, when the flight crew discovers that their flight is carrying the International Pilgrim Virgin Statue, they insist that She move from coach to the First Class cabin, a spectacle that is quite moving to see!

On this particular flight to Europe, I had a connection in Detroit. Upon my arrival I went looking for my gate, and I found it so full of people that I went across to an area where there no one was seated. I had not even sat down when a woman who worked for the airline walked up to me, and said, "Sir, can you tell me what you have in there?" as she pointed to the case with the Statue. My first thought was one of fright: "Oh my goodness, she's some kind of security agent. What's she going to ask me this time?" She went on, "Is that a set of golf clubs or a cello?" I said, "Neither, it's a Statue." She said, surprised, "It's a Statue?" I said, "Yes, it is. It's a Statue of the Blessed Mother." She replied, "Is that right? Can I see Her?" I answered, "Certainly!" So I unzipped up the case and the woman said, "Wow! Look at that! Let me explain. I was standing over there with my friend. See her over there? And when you came walking by, we both looked at each other and wondered what was in the case. I don't know why I decided to come over here and ask you that. It was a bit out of place because I had no reason."

Then she started asking me about the Statue. She told me that she was not Catholic, but when I started telling her about the Statue, she was very impressed. She asked me, "Can I pray to this Statue? Is it OK if I say a prayer before this Statue?" I said, "Sure that's what She's here for." So she thanked me for letting her see the Statue, and then she left. One minute later, her friend came over and said, "Could I see the Statue? My friend told me about her, and we are very moved. If we had never asked, we would have not known about the Statue. Can I say a prayer also? I said, "Of course!" She said, "Because I am trying to have a baby, so I'd like to pray." I said, "There is something very special about this Statue: just ask Her." So it was very touching to see how, in the middle of an airport, two women who were not even Catholic had an intuition that there was something special about the Statue and made a personal inquiry. They said that it wasn't normal that they would ask someone to see what was in their luggage.

Soon I boarded my flight to Amsterdam and in Amsterdam I had to go through customs and walk through the enormous airport. I had a two hour layover before the flight to Vienna so, as I customarily do, I arrived at the gate and opened up the case to say my prayers while looking at the Statue. It is real grace and privilege to be so close to Her, and to be able to meditate and pray in Her presence at any time. I didn't realize, however, that people were paying attention to the Statue while I was praying.

In any case, while everyone else was boarding I was required to wait at the gate and to board last due to some complications with the Statue and my ticket. Normally, I am able to board first to stow the Statue. This time, however, the plane was completely full. As I was walking down the aisle toward the very back, I noticed a row of three seats, one of which was occupied by a man in his fifties with long disheveled hair who didn't look like the most devotional type. It was then that I realized the two empty seats next to the man in the same row were mine.

I expected some problems with him because he looked like a business-man who would be annoyed at being asked to move out of the way to let me through with the Statue, but as I got closer, I saw the man start to grin and become excited. His head started to bob up and down. I then said to him: "Excuse me, sir, but I have to get in there." Much to my surprise, the man, with a huge grin on his face, popped out of his seat and exclaimed, "How can I help you? This is fantastic!" I said, "No, thank you, I can get Her in here" as I entered the row and buckled the Statue in the seat and sat down. I was completely exhausted.

The man looked at me and said in excellent English with a slight accent, "I can't believe this! This is the Madonna! The Madonna is next to me here!" I said, "You know about Her? You're Catholic?" He replied, "Yes, I'm Catholic. The Madonna! I can't believe it! I'm on a business trip, so when I saw her in the airport, and I was shocked out of my shoes to see in the airport a statue of Our Lady!" His enthusiasm deeply touched me. He continued, "Then I get on the airplane, and the Madonna is in the seat next to me! I don't think anything is by coincidence."

The man began to tell me his life story right there in the back of the airplane: he was away from the faith; he was married to a Catholic; his children were raised Catholic but he didn't practice regularly, etc. He also asked me many questions about the faith. So during the hour-and-a-half flight to Vienna, even though I was extremely tired and ready to collapse, I went over all the man's questions and objections and encouraged him to come back to the Church. He was so moved that the Statue was there and was seriously inclined to return to the practice of his faith and religion. He asked for a picture and offered any kind of help that he could give me. In essence, the Statue really touched his life on that one trip, and he said he was going to see how he could change his life because he felt that it was not a coincidence that the Pilgrim Virgin Statue had come to sit in the seat next to him. As our discussion continued, two ladies in the seats in front of us turned around and said, "Excuse us for eavesdropping but, we couldn't help overhearing your conversation. We're Catholic too. We're from Amer-ica. Can we also have a picture of the Statue? We are just impressed that this Statue is with us here." So I said, "Ok, when you get off the plane, wait for me, and I will give you a picture."

EVERYTHING ALWAYS WORKS OUT WITH MARY ON BOARD

The story doesn't end there, however. Whenever I escort the miraculous Statue, my travels don't always go smoothly, but everything always works out in the end. After this pilgrimage, the return flight from Austria to the United States was another opportunity for more such transformations of hearts, but with an unexpected group. The flight was similar to my 1981 trip from Charles De Gaulle Airport to JFK, but this time the flight crew was overwhelmingly won over by the Statue from the start.

When I went to check in at the Vienna airport the "extra seat" provision for the Statue caused a bit of chaos. I was connecting through some European airlines that weren't familiar with this arrangement and thankfully I arrived early. Although it should have taken me only five minutes to check in, it took nearly an hour because they didn't know how to manage the extra seat purchased for the Statue. They performed some "special tricks" on the computer, they said, in order to get the reservations right, and we were eventually able to board our flight to Amsterdam where we would catch our flight back to the United States.

When we landed in Amsterdam, however, it became apparent that they had not corrected the problem! On the flight from Amsterdam to Detroit they had put us in two different seats – not even in the same row – and this never happens. The custodian always sits next to Her on every flight. Someone had bungled the reservations, and I had to correct it at the nearest ticket counter as soon as possible. When the person behind the counter pulled up my record she said: "Oh, everything was done wrong. They messed up over there." That was apparent to me by this time.

It took another forty-five minutes at this counter to correct the problem and soon my patience was starting to wear thin. I was also getting nervous about catching the plane to Detroit. They re-booked the entire reservation, and when she handed me only one boarding pass, she said, "You won't need a boarding pass for the Statue; in fact, you can't have one because it's not a person." I accepted at face value what she said even though it was contrary to what they told me in the morning. "Ok," I said, "as long as I get on the plane and the Statue is next to me." She assured me that this would be the case.

At this point I had to race to the airplane because I had lost nearly an hour getting the tickets straightened out. When I was approaching the counter to board the plane, I showed the gate agent my boarding pass and ticket, and the lady said "Where is your other ticket?" I said "Look, I don't have another ticket; I have a seat for the Statue. They took my other ticket and gave me only this boarding pass for myself. They assured me that a seat was blocked off for the Statue." But the agent responded, "No, you can't get on without the other ticket." I threw up my hands and the equally frustrated attendant went to talk with the manager. However, both of them soon came back and said, "We understand that everything is all set and you can board." Finally!

As we boarded the plane I didn't realize that the tickets I had in my hand were something special. I showed my ticket as I entered the doorway and instead of signaling me to proceed to the right into the cabin, the flight attendant directed us to the left. The Statue and I sat in adjacent seats in business class. Needless to say, I was very surprised that we had been moved up, but I recognized Our Lady's hand in this; I had seen this dynamic before. I was placing the seatbelt on the Statue's case when one of the flight attendants came over and asked, "Oh, what is that, is that a cello?" I said, "No, this is a Statue," and with that her whole demeanor changed. The lady looked at me and said with interest, "Oh, a statue." And I said "Yes, it's a Statue of the Blessed Mother." With that, her interest seemed to grow even greater, and she exclaimed, "What?" I responded, "Yes, this is one of the most famous Statues of the Roman Catholic Church, and it is here on pilgrimage. It's a miraculous Statue."

I immediately launched into the story about the Pilgrim Virgin, and she was quite moved by the details. She told me that she was Catholic and then asked, "Well, can I see the Statue?" "But of course!" I said. When I opened the top part of the Statue case to reveal the face, head, and shoulders, she was just overwhelmed by Our Lady's beauty. She ran and told several of her co-workers about it and before long I had five other flight attendants wanting to see the Statue. They too were very impressed by the story of the Statue and were asking all kinds of questions about Fatima, about the Statue, and commenting about what a grace it was to have Her on their flight. At a certain point they had to go on with their work but very shortly after that, one of the flight attendants came back to make a point of telling me, "I'm overwhelmed to know that this Statue is on board. I have goose bumps that She's here with us."

One of the most beautiful things that happened came just a few minutes before take-off. At a certain point the flight was full, and one of the ground managers came into business class to see if he could find one more place for a last passenger. He said to the flight attendants, "Let's move this Statue and put it in the closet so we can give that seat to the passenger." Before I could say anything, three or four of the flight crew convened on the man and said, "No, no, no! She has to stay here. She can't go. We'll give up our seats for Her. We will sit in the jump seats if necessary." The crew usually reserve regular seats for taking naps on long, international flights, but the pull-down jump seats, which are used for domestic flights, are nonetheless available. These ladies insisted that they would give up their seats in order to keep the Pilgrim Virgin Statue in place. I wouldn't have allowed it anyway, but the generosity of the flight attendants was simply magnificent. They eventually found another seat for the passenger and that settled the issue. One of the stewardesses came by and patted me on the arm and said, "Wow that was close, but it's going to work out now." Little did she know that this was our motto: "With Our Lady everything works out in the end."

There was a delay of about an hour before takeoff which gave time for the whole crew to come over and talk with me. At one point eight or nine crew members packed into the somewhat restricted space in business class, and they were all asking about the Statue and asking for pictures. One-by-one each of the crew members came up to me, and I gave each of them pictures that I had touched to the Statue. Many of them used the opportunity to tell me their personal stories, one of the most satisfying aspects of the whole experience. One of flight attendants, who happened to be the head of the crew, a man in his thirties, told me that he prays the Rosary with his grandmother when he's home. They wanted to give me donations, but I told them that wasn't necessary. Instead, they asked if they could be part of our Fatima campaign and sign up on our mailing list, so I took their names and addresses to send them a Fatima book and other literature when I returned home.

Throughout the remainder of the flight back to Detroit the crew members kept coming by wanting to see the Statue again. They were simply mesmerized by the gaze of Our Lady. I asked if one of them had a flash light, and when they handed me one, I focused the beam on the face of

Our Lady which made for a remarkable image in the darkened cabin. I told them how privileged they were to be that close to the Statue, and they certainly agreed with me.

Upon our arrival, I told them that we could take a group picture with the Statue, and I promised to send them a copy of it with the Fatima literature. They were delighted at that and thanked me very much as they left the plane. The captain, copilot, and navigator also came back to see the Statue because they had heard about it but were unable to come back to see it during the flight. They were very moved by the Statue's beauty, and the captain, who told me he was Catholic, asked me for a picture. We took the Statue to the first class cabin and took a picture with the captain and the crew members, which I later sent to them. They were extremely grateful for the experience and couldn't thank me enough for having brought the Statue on board their plane. They said it was a great blessing to have had the occasion to accompany the Pilgrim Virgin Statue on that leg of the trip and reiterated that they were looking forward to receiving information on the Statue and the pilgrimages.

Before I deplaned with the Statue, the captain told me that this was the most important "passenger" he had ever had on a flight! A week after arriving home, I received the following email from him, which I think sums up Our Lady's transformative grace:

Dear Thomas:

I just returned home from my trip with Northwest and showed my wife and boys the picture of Our Lady. I want to say thank you on behalf of my crew. Thank you again for staying after the flight to show us the statue. I have never seen anything that can compare to it and her face is still visible to me in my mind. The large photo was slightly damaged during my travel but it will be framed and placed in a prominent place in my home. I would be very interested in any info about how to have the statue in our parish. Thanks so much for the memory of this.

Sincerely Yours,

Tom Perillo

Northwest Captain

As I was finishing this book, I re-read the email from the pilot and felt inspired to follow up with him about our encounter fourteen years earlier. In doing so, I learned that, sadly, he had only recently passed away after a long battle with Lyme disease.

I was able, however, to contact Captain Perillo's wife, Diane, through the local parish priest who attested to the pilot's deep faith. Diane vividly recalled the day that her husband came home from that transatlantic flight and told her and their three sons about the encounter with Our Lady on the airplane. Diane said that they had in fact framed the picture of the statue I had given him and that it remained on their dresser near their bed to this very day, even after her husband's passing. In talking with her I learned that Capt. Perillo was a devout Catholic throughout his entire life and that Our Lady had always been central to his faith, epecially in the last year of his life as he suffered with the fatal disease.

She told of their regular habit of praying the Rosary together and explained what a grace it was to have his three adult sons at home with them during the last six weeks of their father's life. She said that he specifically took the opportunity to discuss his deep faith with each of the boys and that the whole family would spend the evenings together talking, praying and singing in the company of their father.

The night he passed away his wife recalled: "Tom was in a hospital bed with a breathing apparatus. That evening we noticed that he was trying to tell us something and finally we understood that he was saying that he had seen Mary. He said She was just smiling at him. He passed away that night in his sleep. Afterwards I thought, I should have known he would pass that night. It was a great consolation for me and my sons that Our Lord sent His mother to bring Tom home."

It was inspiring to see that the sincere Marian devotion that Capt. Perillo nurtured throughout his life had provided him with profound consolation from Our Blessed Mother at his time of death. I thought it very significant and recalled what he had written to me in the email fourteen years earlier after seeing the Pilgrim Virgin on the plane: "...*her face is still visible to me in my mind.*"

As we were ending our conversation Diane recounted an inspiring story about her husband that I found admirable. She explained that for the last several years of his career, before the illness, he had served as the Chief Pilot for Northwest Airlines in Minneapolis. As Chief Pilot he oversaw the pilot training progrmas and other related matters. One day, a certain pilot that Tom had taken under his wing was taking his flight check test in the flight simulator, and Tom was worried that the man might not pass the test. It was a known fact that Tom had left his office that afternoon and gone to the flight simulator where he stood on the catwalk overhead praying the Rosary for the pilot's success. Needless to say, the pilot passed the test.

EXTERNAL CHANGES REQUIRE INNER RENEWAL

Despite the many wonders that Our Lady can perform on the world stage, She is nonetheless a *purveyor of God's grace* and not a magician. She will not – in fact *cannot* – force people to accept God's offer of salvation through repentance. Coercion is not Her way because it is not God's way. His invitation to life always passes through the free will of the individual without violating the innermost core of the human person's dignity and responsibility. Grace moves hearts, grace disposes people toward God, but the human will is the ultimate arbiter of the individual's eternal salvation. God "wills everyone to be saved and to come to knowledge of the truth" (1 Pt 2:4), but He does not force people to join His wedding banquet; and neither does Our Lady.

John Haffert remarked in one of his publications that "miracles in themselves do not cause conversions."[119] And he is right. There is always a need for personal faith, even in the face of miraculous interventions. The Administrator of the municipality of Ourem, Arturo Santos, is a good example of the human ability to nullify God's grace. He was the one who had been responsible for kidnapping and imprisoning the three children in August of 1917 so that they missed the apparition of Our Lady that month. He added to his crimes the outrageous threat, delivered with vehemence to each of the three children, that he would have them boiled in oil if they did not reveal the secret of Our Lady. His treatment of the children can only be interpreted as an act of willful and malicious torture of the innocent. Santos outlived the incident by nearly four decades and died in June of 1955 after a quiet retire-

119   John M. Haffert, *Queen's Promise* (Washington, New Jersey: Ave Maria Institute, 1966), 57.

ment, never renouncing his atheistic attitudes, and never (openly) repenting of his behavior during the 1917 events.

Worse, this man who had greater evidence of the truth of the apparitions and saw more closely than anyone else the purity of the witnesses, died refusing the last sacraments when they were offered. One account of him before his passing indicated that he had been present in 1942 when the original statue processed by his village on the way to Lisbon. On that occasion he was heard to have declared, "I am not at all in favor of religion and of priests… but when I saw the image of the vision I felt inwardly something which I cannot explain…."[120] Was Our Lady trying to touch Santos' heart even in 1942, giving him a chance to repent before he died? We can only hope. Nevertheless, Santos offered scant evidence of any real change. King Herod, too, was fascinated by the message that John the Baptist preached (Mk 6:14-29) and he beheld the Holy One with his own eyes (Lk 23:6-12), but there is no evidence that Herod ever repented.

Likewise, the changes that even *millions of people* pray for do not always occur because the grace of God can be blocked by the viciousness of unrepentant hearts. In Chapter 6 we spoke of the month-long prayer for peace in Vietnam which culminated in the February 1974 Pilgrim Virgin's visit. Countless millions of people of all faiths prayed for peace in the war-torn Vietnam and no fewer than two million people, including the President of the Republic at that time, came to welcome the Statue for the closing ceremonies. However, the following year Mr. Haffert wrote an article in Soul magazine entitled, "What Happened to the 'Miracle' in Vietnam?" In the article he expressed tangible disappointment that the fruits of Her visit were not more evident:

What happened to the "miracle" which so many ardently and confidently expected just one year ago? Peace has not come. And Congressman Do Sinh Tu, who had been the primary force behind that crusade of prayer, was almost beaten to death eight months later by government police when he intervened on behalf of some anti-corruption demonstrators in Saigon![121]

---

120   Ibid., 61, Note. This story was recounted by the Portuguese religious Magazine, *Stella*, in December of 1955, after Santos died.

121   J.M. Haffert, "What Happened to the 'Miracle' in Vietnam?" Soul Magazine, March-April 1975.

The expected miracle transformation did not happen, but it was certainly not due to any fault on the part of Heaven. In the very month that Mr. Haffert was writing, plans were being made for the final withdrawal of American troops from that country, which created the power vacuum into which the atheistic Communist forces only too happily entered. Vietnam remains a Communist country to this day.

Nonetheless it would be a mistake to think that so much prayer is without its effect, even among the hardest of hearts. God's grace runs like water through the prayers of a nation and flows to the places where it is allowed to go. One tangible grace was the Fatima Shrine outside of Saigon that was built as a result of the Statue's visit; it is a place of prayer that has inspired and consoled millions in their suffering. Moreover, despite the worsening political situation after the American withdrawal, one of the most remarkable results of Our Lady's visit after that month of prayer was the reversal of South Vietnam's abortion and birth control laws.[122] St. Paul said in his letter to the Romans, "Where sin increased, grace overflowed all the more" (Rom 5:20), and the vibrant Catholic faith of the Vietnamese to this day is a testimony to how marvelously the fluid grace of God in Our Lady's hands can transform people and societies – even when it has to flow around hearts of stone.

---

122   Ibid.

REVERSING THE REBELLION OF SATAN

*The two great forces of the Mystical Body of Christ
and the Mystical Body of the Antichrist are beginning to draw up their
battle lines for the catastrophic combat.*
~Archbishop Fulton J. Sheen, in *Communism
and the Conscience of the West*, 1951.

*T*wenty million people died of a single deadly disease in the Soviet Union in the last century. The same disease killed *sixty-five million* in China. It also violently snuffed out the lives of two million people in both Cambodia and North Korea, and added more than five million deaths in Afghanistan, the Eastern Bloc countries, Ethiopia, and Vietnam.[123]

What massive disease killed more than ninety-four million people in the course of the 20th Century?

Atheistic Communism.

In fact, the Black Plague in the 14th Century was less deadly than the pestilence of 20th Century Communism. It is estimated that the Bubonic Plague that raged through Europe from 1347 onward killed close to 60% of the entire population of the continent; that is, nearly fifty million people.[124] But the Black Plague was a natural disaster: atheistic Communism is a spiritual one.

Before Communism became rooted in Western Europe as a political force, Our Lady appeared in Portugal and warned Her listeners with abso-

123   These statistics are taken from Stephen Courtois et al., *The Black Book of Communism* (Cambridge: Harvard University Press, 1997), 2-4.

124   Ole J. Benedictow, "The Black Death: The Greatest Catastrophe Ever," *History Today*, Vol. 55, Issue 3, March, 2005. http://www.historytoday.com/ole-j-benedictow/black-death-greatest-catastrophe-ever.

lute clarity that the spread of "the errors of Russia" would be an unprecedented calamity for both the Church and the world. She spoke a message to the children in July of 1917 that neither they nor most of the world at that time could possibly have understood but only taken on faith: *"If my requests are not granted, Russia will spread her errors throughout the world, provoking wars and persecutions of the Church. The good will be martyred, the Holy Father will have much to suffer, and various nations will be annihilated!"* A full century after the fact, we are more aware today of what Our Lady meant by "the spread of errors" from Russia than the people of 1917 could possibly have understood.

WHAT ERRORS? ·

Any attempt to catalogue the errors of Russia must take into account the three spiritual principles upon which the ideology of a Marxist/Communist[125] state rests. I will not attempt to offer a comprehensive picture of Marxism as a philosophical or political system here. My aim is to show the philosophy's *spiritual* dimension which preceded and worked itself into various political systems in the 20th century, a number of which survive to the present day. Moreover, it is important to note that even where the political systems failed, the intellectual and social manifestations of Marxism are alive and well in our world and continuing to spread their "errors", as Our Lady predicted.

1. Atheism:

By singling out Russia in Her message, Our Lady meant to expose the dangers of an atheistic system of government that not only nullifies God's sovereignty over the world but attempts to eradicate the very concept of Him in human hearts and minds. Atheistic Communism's attempt to systematically eliminate God from public and private life was a wholly destructive force that was entering the world in the very year that Our Lady appeared in

---

125   The term Marxist derives from the philosophical progenitor of Communism, the German philosopher Karl Marx (1818-1883), whose main works, *The Communist Manifesto* (1848) and *Das Kapital* (1867), gave the world the philosophical basis for what we call "Communism".

Fatima. Mr. Haffert noted that the real problem of the Russia that Our Lady spoke about was not its Communists per se, many of whom were sincere but misguided. The real problem is atheism, which is not limited to Russia. "That is why we believe the message of Fatima never mentions this confusing name [Communism] by which Marxists have chosen to be known.... It is to be realized that the atheists, on the other hand believe that they...not we...are concerned with saving the world."[126] Russia and "the errors of Russia" were, in Mr. Haffert's mind, metaphors for the spread of godless atheism in any form throughout the world.

2. Violations of Human Rights and Dignity:

The second dimension of "the errors of Russia" is its denial of the inherent rights and dignity of the human person. Christianity was nearly a thousand years old in Russia by the time the Bolsheviks took over, so Communist efforts to eradicate the Christian worldview from the heart of Mother Russia required the imposition of harsh and systematic tyrannical injustices upon masses of people over a great period of time. The sufferings experienced by citizens of Communist states includes a long list of inhumane acts: arbitrary executions; persecution of clergy and the often violent suppression of religious practice and education; imprisonment of innocent individuals in concentration camps without due cause; social engineering through involuntary deportation of entire ethnic groups; man-made famines and the forced starvation of millions. Our Lady spoke to us at Fatima about wars and persecutions, the martyrdom of the good, and the suffering that the Holy Father would endure on account of the evils spinning out of control in a world influenced by Communism.

3. Materialism:

A world without God is also a flat, two-dimensional world that holds all the beauty of a barren desert landscape. It is a world focused on *things*, without hope for something beyond the illusory "progress" of humanity. The atheistic doctrine of materialism creates an earth without a heaven. And because it lacks a spiritual dimension, materialism also creates a world with many idols to worship instead of the True God. This false mindset

126   Haffert, *Russia Converted*, 10.

is not limited to Communism but has infiltrated the West as well. In an address in 2007 Pope Benedict XVI noted:

> today, more than in the past, the education and formation of the person are influenced by…a mindset and culture marked by relativism, consumerism and a false and destructive exaltation, or rather, profanation, of the body and of sexuality.[127]

Indeed there are many false gods, and no culture or political system has a monopoly on idol worship.

A PILGRIMAGE OF FAITH WITH OUR LADY

The Pan Am flight that I described in Chapter 1 was the culmination of a pilgrimage that I undertook with members of the TFP in Europe in 1981. As mentioned, my colleague Paul Folley and I retrieved the Statue from its restorers in Madrid and brought it to France. The motive of our trip was simple. We wanted to bring the Pilgrim Virgin Statue to various historic sites that were important in the history of Christian Europe to ask Our Lady's intercession to protect Christian Europe from the many dangers on the horizon. The early Eighties saw a renewal of interest in socialism in various countries of Europe, France above all. The newly-elected President of that country, Francois Mitterand, had launched a new socialist program disguised under the deceptive term, "Self-Managing Socialism," which threatened to further disintegrate the Catholic character of France. This was the exact danger that Our Lady warned about at Fatima; Mitterand's "new socialism" was actually quite old and tired. It was just another attempt to spread "the errors of Russia" to the country known as the First-Born (or Eldest) Daughter of the Church.

France's title was well-earned. Most people associate France with the great Emperor Charlemagne (742-814), which is accurate to a degree. He was head of the Frankish kingdom and ruled over a portion of the continent

127   Pope Benedict XVI, Inauguration of the Convention of the Diocese of Rome, Basilica of Saint John Lateran, 6/11/07.

that incorporated much of Western and Central Europe. He was declared the undisputed leader in Europe by Pope Leo III, who crowned him the *Imperator Augustus* on Christmas Day in the year 800. Charlemagne is the founder of both the French and German monarchies and is rightly regarded as the Father of Europe. He was a thoroughly Catholic king and presided over a renaissance in Western Europe that fused the entire continent into what was thereafter known as "Christendom," literally, the Kingdom of Christ. The cultural, economic, and spiritual renaissance of the 8th and 9th Centuries took on the name Carolingian to signify Charlemagne as its primary patron and inspiration.

A THRONE OF GRACE

The City of Aachen, Germany was the actual seat of Charlemagne's empire. Pope Leo dedicated a chapel in honor of the Blessed Virgin Mary in the Emperor's castle which served as the place of consecration for kings and emperors of Europe for the next six hundred years. The Emperor and his family assisted Holy Mass in a royal space reserved in the upper gallery of the chapel, in which was situated a simple, austere, stone throne for the Emperor while he attended services. It was this throne that was the special object of our pilgrimage. Our aim was to place the Pilgrim Virgin Statue upon *Charlemagne's throne* as a symbolic gesture to ask Her to preserve the Christian civilization that was once inspired and defended from this sacred site. It was a grand ambition but not necessarily a practical one.

When our small group of pilgrims arrived at the chapel with the Statue in 1981, the attendants asked us what we were doing. One of the guards there told us that it was absolutely forbidden to touch the throne or even get too near to it. Normally this would have discouraged a simple pilgrim, but we were with the Queen herself. My companions explained to him the history and significance of Our Lady's Statue, and our presentation must have been persuasive because he soon allowed us to place the Statue upon Charlemagne's throne. He made an extremely rare exception. But we were with Our Lady who opens doors to hearts, and we understood that Her grace was operative in that sacred place.

I was filled with a sense of wonder as I stepped back and viewed the scene: on the same throne from which a great Catholic king once ruled Europe, the image of the Queen of Heaven and Earth was now sitting. My companions and I knelt down to pray right there in the gallery of the chapel. We prayed that She would watch over and protect the civilization that had once been Christian Europe and restore it to its original dignity and beauty. We prayed that one day Europe would be re-united under the banner of the One, True Catholic Faith again and free of the menacing threat of Communism and its deceptive cousin socialism which Our Lady had spoken of. I remember being very moved by this scene and all it represented, despite the fact that Europe was entering a period of experimentation with socialism that was to have the predictable devastating effects that had been witnessed already throughout the 20th Century: atheism, materialism, and the denial of basic human rights (through increasing liberalization of abortion, euthanasia, so-called gay rights, etc.).

Later we would witness the reality of French socialism gone wild. During the decades of the Eighties and Nineties Pope John Paul II continually exhorted the leaders of the European Union to include references to God and Christianity in the revision of their charters, but by 2007 – the fiftieth anniversary of its founding – the EU had excluded any mention of God or Christian foundations in the European Union's Constitution. Its rejection was primarily spearheaded by the French: "Plans to include such a reference in the original EU treaty," said a Reuters news service article, "rejected by French and Dutch voters in 2005, were blocked by French President Jacques Chirac."[128] The atheists had defeated Charlemagne.

Or had they? One very tangible result of that pilgrimage, however, was the immense increase and flowering of the Fatima network in Europe, particularly in France, a network that remains active to this day. In Our Lady's hands, God's grace once again flowed around those hearts of stone. There are also signs of a growing pro-life movement in recent years. The French have sponsored a national March for Life, since 2005 and in 2014 more than half a million people marched in Paris against so-called gay rights laws and in defense of the natural family.[129]

128   Philip Pullella, "Pope criticizes EU for excluding God," Reuters, 3/24/07; http://www.reuters.com/article/us-eu-anniversary-pope-idUSL2421365520070324.

129   Jeanne Smits, "Hundreds of thousands join march in Paris supporting natural family," LifeSiteNews, 10/01/14; https://www.lifesitenews.com/opinion/hundreds-of-thousands-join-march-in-par-

THE ABBEY AND THE CITY OF LIGHTS

Among the many other sites we visited on the pilgrimage was the former Benedictine abbey of Cluny (pron. Clue-Nee) where, during the centuries following the reign of Charlemagne the monks carried out a renewal of monastic life, liturgy, piety, art, architecture, and learning that has come to be known as the Reform of Cluny. All of this took place in what secular historians slanderously term the Dark Ages. For France, these centuries were anything but dark. The abbey was founded in 910 by St. Odo of Cluny and spread its reform throughout France and into England, Spain and Italy. By the 12th Century the Cluny Congregation included more than a thousand monasteries. Over the next several centuries Cluny produced saints, statesmen, and even four popes from among its ranks of monks. Cluny inspired a literal renaissance of the Catholic Faith both in the religious and secular spheres. It is hard to overestimate the impact of the abbey of Cluny on European Catholicism.

During the sinister and bloody French Revolution seven hundred years later, the abbey of Cluny was destroyed – a grim testimony to the satanic and destructive urge of atheistic ideology. I vividly remember processing through the venerable ruins of the ancient abbey with the Statue of Our Lady and praying to the Blessed Mother to bring about (another) renaissance of the spirit of the Church that had once radiated from Cluny throughout the whole of Christendom.

Our next and final stop was Paris, the famed City of Lights where we spent several days before returning to the United States. It was in Paris that we learned of a large-scale protest campaign being launched by the global network of TFP organizations aimed at denouncing and exposing the socialist threat inaugurated by President Francois Mitterrand of France. Knowing that the greatest evils perpetrated by the devil are no match for Our Blessed Mother, we decided to go with the Pilgrim Virgin Statue to many of the significant places in the city of Paris where the revolutionaries had committed great atrocities against the Church and the Christian civilization it had

is-supporting-natural-family.

formed. True to the Fatima message, we were making a pilgrimage of reparation for the sins committed during the French Revolution. This was about as amazing an experience as I could possibly have had as a twenty-year-old whose life experience up to that point had pretty much been that of the rural city in Southern California where I grew up.

We set out on this special act of reparation during the wee hours of the night. We traveled in a caravan of several cars to the significant spots of the Revolution, and at each spot the occupants of the cars got out, displayed the Statue uncovered before the site of the atrocity, and prayed deeply that Our Mother would intercede for humanity and inspire the Triumph of Her Immaculate Heart. We begged Her to thwart and undo the scourge of socialism and Communism that She warned about at Fatima. The most moving experience of the entire pilgrimage for me was at the Place de la Concorde in the very center of Paris where we prayed near the actual location of the beheading of King Louis XVI by the revolutionary mob in 1793. It is said that his royal blood ran down the street and mingled with that of many of his fellow countrymen, and his death brought an end to the French monarchy of Charlemagne. As I prayed, I could not help but think of the many millions of victims of atheistic Communism that would be killed in a similar fashion more than two centuries later by the same unholy spirit of the Antichrist that was unleashed during the French Revolution.

We finished our pilgrimage of reparation with the International Pilgrim Virgin Statue in Paris and prepared for our return flight to JFK international airport in New York.

OUR LADY'S ONGOING INVITATION

These *systems of rebellion* and the individual acts of sin that create them "offend God very much," said Our Lady of Fatima to the three shepherd children in Her final apparition. But Our Lady wastes no time in lamenting sin; She does something about it. She invited the children to be part of the solution to this heinous rebellion: "Are you willing to offer yourselves to God and bear all the sufferings He wills to send you, as an act of reparation for the sins by which He is offended and in supplication for the conversion of sinners?"

Our Lady's concern for the outrages, sacrileges, and indifference which offend God has not diminished in the least. In fact, now that the errors of Russia have spread throughout the entire world, Her invitation for us to become the antidote to these offenses has only become more urgent. Her goal is nothing less than to reverse the revolution of Satan. But is our generation listening to Her plea?

ENLIVENING THE FAITHFUL OF THE WORLD

As [the Pilgrim Statue] tours America, Europe, Africa and India,
Indonesia and Australia, blessings pour down from heaven and marvels of
grace multiply in such a way that we can hardly believe what our eyes are see-
ing.... Under the maternal gaze of the heavenly Pilgrim, no antagonism
of nationality or race is divisive, no diversity of borders separates,
no conflict of interest causes dissention; everybody, at every
moment, feels happy to look at one another as brothers.
~Pope Pius XII, Papal Audience, October 13th, 1951.

*J*ohn Haffert was a humble man. He proved it by the way he handled the Pilgrim Virgin Statue's inaugural mission to North America. It was Mr. Haffert's dream and his greatest desire that the Statue should come to New York first and be crowned in the United States as a fitting initiation for Her missionary work. That, after all, was the reason he had the Statue made. This Statue, in particular, was the very one (out of the four Thedim statues) that was destined to tour North America and create a force of prayer for the fulfillment of Our Lady's wishes for the conversion of Russia. The Pilgrim Virgin Statue and the European statue were intended to be reunited in the capital of the Soviet Union bringing all the prayers of Catholics around the world with them. How disappointed he was that his plan for the Pilgrim Virgin Statue was altered by the Archbishop of New York.

Mr. Haffert was one of the most proactive men on the planet; he undoubtedly fit the classic description of the man with a mission. In his enthusiasm and devotion to Our Lady, he worked fast and rarely consulted about the decisions he felt needed to be taken. In the case of the Pilgrim Virgin Statue's arrival, this turned out to be a problem. Apparently, he neglected Church protocol by failing to consult with His Eminence, Francis Cardinal Spellman, before he planned to bring the Statue to New York. Mr. Haffert frankly admitted that it never occurred to him that such a marvelous event should need anyone's permission![130] As a result, he was informed that Cardinal Spellman had reservations about the Statue coming to his Archdiocese when it arrived in the US. And perhaps there was more than a protocol issue behind the matter. Cardinal Spellman apparently was reluctant because he believed that parading a statue of the Virgin Mary in public would offend Protestants. Be that as it may, the Statue was not crowned initially in the United States or allowed to tour the Archdiocese of New York at that time, and Mr. Haffert humbly complied with the wishes of the Church's authority. I believe that he received a blessing in return because the Statue was welcomed with open arms in Canada and a few weeks later was able to come to the United States – but through the back door, so to speak. Truly with Our Lady, all things work out in the end.

THE STATUE'S FIRST STOP – CANADA

With New York a closed book, the Pilgrim Virgin was invited to the Canadian dioceses of Ottawa, Hamilton, Montreal, Toronto, and Quebec in Her inaugural pilgrimage of faith. The Statue's first tour lasted forty-nine days, and it is hard to overestimate the type of reception that She received among Catholics in Canada at that time. An impressive amount of writing and reporting was done around that event, but it will be impossible to cite all the sources and details of the trip. The first fervor of faith, however, needs to be documented to show how many seeds of the Gospel were planted in that fertile Canadian soil.

The Pilgrim Virgin Statue left Portugal on October 13th, 1947 and was brought to the United States by Canon José Galamba de Oliveira, the Vicar General of the Diocese of Leiria-Fatima. He was accompanied by John Haffert, the Statue's founder and originator. When the Statue was brought through US Customs for the first time, it was necessary to declare owner-

130   Haffert, *Brother and I*, 170-71.

ship of the Statue and while John Haffert wanted the Statue to belong to the Bishop of Fatima, Canon Oliveira insisted that Haffert's name be put on the papers attesting that he owned the Statue. This established Mr. Haffert as the legal owner of the Statue until the day it was finally deeded by Mrs. Haffert to the Blue Army on September 1st, 2014.[131]

In those days there were no non-stop transatlantic commercial flights so the Statue's first stop was in the Azores, an archipelago of nine islands due west of Portugal in the mid-Atlantic, for a several hour layover and refueling. In Her very first trip outside of Fatima, a group of faithful were already following Her progress and were waiting for Her at the island's tiny airport. They had obtained from their government the highly unusual permission to board an international flight while still on the tarmac in order to venerate Her and to pray before the Blessed Virgin's image inside the airplane.[132] Upon landing at La Guardia Airport in New York, the Statue was taken to the home of John Haffert on Long Island for an overnight stay before leaving for Ottawa by car the next day. When they arrived at the Canadian border to cross the Rainbow Bridge into Prescott, Canada, an astounding 10,000 people were waiting in miserable weather to greet the Statue.[133]

The Archbishop of Ottawa, His Excellency Alexander Vachon, received the Statue with all due solemnity at the border. "Archbishop Vachon," wrote Mr. Haffert, "waiting in gold cope and miter, walked majestically through the rain with his entourage to meet the car, then proceeded into customs. The line of cars escorting the statue to Ottawa from the border was thirty miles long."[134] The first prayer event took place at the stadium of the local university, where some *100,000 faithful* witnessed the solemn and official crowning of the Pilgrim Statue of Fatima by the archbishop. This crowning was the main event of Our Lady's entry into North America. Nearly two hundred priests were present, who, together with the people, knelt with the Archbishop to recite the act of consecration to the Immaculate Heart of Mary. Incredibly, at midnight, 124 churches throughout the diocese celebrated Masses

131   Haffert Interview of 4/27/99 and http://wafusa.org/the-apostolate/national-pilgrim-virgin-statue/.

132   "Our Lady of Fatima Comes to America," *The Scapular* Magazine, November-December, 1947.

133   "Thousands of Pilgrims Defy Weather to Revere Catholic Replica Statue," *Niagara Falls Gazette*, 10/20/47.

134   Ibid.

simultaneously in honor of Our Lady's visit and for Her intentions: reparation for sins, conversion of sinners, etc. Archbishop Vachon's homily at the Cathedral Mass was so much in line with Our Lady of Fatima's message that even the local newspaper, the Ottawa Journal, could not confound his words: "Archbishop Opens Crusade against Deluge of Impurity," read the headline the next day.[135] And that was in 1947! Another headline in Ottawa's French-language newspaper read, "Triómphe à Notre-Dame de Fatima,"[136] a clear allusion to Our Lady's message about the triumph of Her Immaculate Heart.

THE PILGRIM VIRGIN MAKES A
GRAND ENTRANCE INTO THE UNITED STATES

One of the bishops in attendance at the Canadian event was Archbishop John F. O'Hara, CSC, of Buffalo (later Cardinal Archbishop of Philadelphia). He was so impressed with the turnout and the devotion that the Statue inspired that he asked for the Statue to visit his diocese in the United States. Several weeks later, Bishop Joseph Ryan of the Diocese of Hamilton, the last diocese She visited in Canada, commended the Pilgrim Statue into the safekeeping of Archbishop O'Hara, who then brought Her into the United States via the entry at Niagara Falls on December 8th, 1947, the Solemnity of the Immaculate Conception and our nation's patronal feast day. In Chapter 7 we described the cure that was obtained during that visit to Buffalo, but the overwhelming reception of the Statue by the faithful of Buffalo was something altogether extraordinary.

In Buffalo the Statue was met by some 200,000 people, more than one-third of the entire population of the city![137] Even more impressive than the number of people was the number of confessions, communions, and the intense devotion that the people displayed. Our Lady was already, in Her inaugural tour, establishing a pattern for Her missionary journeys: massive crowds; a rousing, joyful welcome; an increase in faith, hope, and charity

135   *Ottawa Journal*, 10/20/47; cf. also, Fr. Hector Legros and Sister Paul-Émile, S.C.O., History of the Archdiocese of Ottawa, *Le Diocèse d'Ottawa* (1847-1948), 1949, 106, for a first-hand account of the event.

136   *Le Droit*, 10/20/47.

137   Haffert, *Russia Converted*, 210; Mary Ryan, "200,000 Americans Welcome Their Queen," The *Scapular* Magazine, January-February, 1948.

among the people; and even undeniable miracles and healings.

Archbishop O'Hara was so amazed at the supernatural manifestations, conversions, and the quality of his people's devotion that he offered to talk to all the bishops of the US when they gathered in Washington, DC shortly after that. Following the lead of Cardinal Spellman, however, very few bishops offered to host a visit of the Statue to their diocese. Providentially, the bishops of Raleigh, North Carolina and Houston, Texas were inspired and soon thereafter invitations from other bishops started pouring in. About a year after Her grand entrance into the US, even Cardinal Spellman allowed Her to visit St. Patrick's Cathedral in New York; and seeing the incredible outpouring of devotion of his diocese for Our Lady, he extended the visit another week.

We can speak, in fact, of a veritable *tidal wave* of Marian devotion that swept the United States in the first year-and-a-half of Her touring. A partial list of the crowds that came to greet our Lady in that time period is simply unbelievable: in the Archdiocese of Boston (30,000); at the National Shrine of Our Lady of Sorrows in Chicago (125,000-150,000); at the University of Notre Dame in Indiana (10,000); in the city of Detroit, Michigan (45,000); in the Diocese of Houston, Texas (15,000); at the Shrine of the Little Flower, San Antonio, Texas (40,000); in the Diocese of Covington, Kentucky (65,000); in the small town of New Iberia, Louisiana (20,000); at Sacred Heart Church in Memphis, Tennessee (10,000); in the Diocese of Corpus Christi, Texas (50,000); and the list goes on.[138]

John Haffert estimated that as many as four million people had seen and touched the Statue in its first year of touring – a number that constituted more than half the population of Portugal at the time.[139] An edition of *Soul* Magazine in 1967, twenty years after the inaugural tour, acknowledged that, in addition to its many international travels, the Pilgrim Virgin Statue had visited 145 dioceses of the United States and Canada and travelled over 700,000 miles in North America alone. Truly Our Lady took the countries of North America by storm and entirely fulfilled the initial vision of Mr. Haffert for a missionary Statue to this continent. As it would be a tedious exercise

---

138   Statistics gleaned from issues of *Soul* Magazine and various other event publications and articles from 1947 and 1949.

139   Haffert, *Russia Converted*, 212.

to recount the specifics of even a fraction of Our Lady's visits during those twenty years of touring, I have chosen to focus only on the highlights of the 1947-48 Buffalo trip (above) and the St. Meinrad events (below) because they are so exemplary.

THE FATIMA WEEK AT ST. MEINRAD

No account of the Pilgrim Virgin Statue's initial visit to the US would be complete if we did not tell the story of how She overwhelmed America's heartland with a week of spiritual exercises at the renowned Benedictine Abbey of St. Meinrad in southern Indiana. In fact, one author called it "the biggest event of its kind since the World's Fair in 1939" and "the World's Fair for Our Lady."[140]

On March 29th, 1948, Abbot Ignatius Esser asked for permission from Archbishop Schulte of Indianapolis for the Pilgrim Statue to visit the Abbey. After some negotiations, the visit of the Pilgrim Statue to St. Meinrad was set for the week of August 14th – 20th and preparations began for what was expected to be an enormous outpouring of enthusiasm from the people of the local area. Little did they realize that word of the visit would spread far and wide and that people would travel from *all over the continental United States* to see the Pilgrim Virgin Statue during that week. The monks prepared the Abbey shrine to receive the crowds and set up an elaborate stage with an altar for open air Masses. They also provided twenty-one confessionals to be manned by thirty priests on rotations during the week.

The nearest town to the Abbey (eighteen miles away) had only 5,000 inhabitants, but more than 120,000 faithful descended on St. Meinrad that week, and there were virtually no accommodations available. People slept in their cars or set up make-shift camping areas on the Abbey grounds for the entire week, something that had never been seen at the remote Benedictine enclave. It is also important to note that this took place at a time when the interstate system had not yet been established and travel was via local highways and roads. The number of faithful, therefore, that traveled to southern Indiana at that time for that event was literally historic.

---

140   Stephen Oraze, "The World's Fair for Our Lady," The Scapular Magazine, January-February, 1949, 2-3, 10-13. The article was condensed from *The Grail* Magazine.

When it came time to retrieve the Statue at the Jesuit house of studies in West Baden Springs (approximately forty miles away), a motorcade of some 750 cars joined the procession, with a police escort in both the front and the back of the line. On the way, crowds gathered at the roadsides to welcome Our Lady, and when they arrived at the Abbey, there were so many people around and inside the church that they had to divert the initial enthronement ceremony to the outside altar. The Statue was carried in procession by a group of monks and placed on the altar in front of the initial crowd of 5,000 people. It is said that every available bus within a radius of one hundred miles was booked for this event alone.

Upon the Statue's arrival, Abbot Esser proceeded with the crowning and enthronement which gave a formal opening to the Fatima Week at St. Meinrad. The schedule of the week was conducted with typical Benedictine rigor: the Abbey bells began ringing at 3:45 am; then, beginning at 4:00 am there were Masses throughout the day every half hour with a Pontifical Mass offered at 10:00 am. Each day a different member of the hierarchy offered the Pontifical Mass. The faithful could attend Marian Hours of Reparation in the Abbey church from 1:00 to 6:00 pm, and another Hour of Reparation at the outdoor altar at 7:00 pm. The days concluded with Night Prayer and veneration of the Statue. There were seven sermons preached daily at the Masses and Holy Hours and more than one hundred Masses offered during the week. The faithful prayed the Rosary publicly six times each day, and needless to say, there was ample opportunity for sacramental confession.

Two highlights of the week deserve special mention. August 15th was the Feast of the Assumption, and at least 25,000 people came to the Abbey for this holy day of obligation. That was a record up to point in the week's festivities. However, on Thursday, August 19th, it was estimated that more than 40,000 pilgrims came to the Abbey, 3,000 of whom were sick or disabled. Most of the sermons of the 19th were about the reality of pain and suffering and how these can be turned into sacrifices when accepted with resignation and a fervent sense of faith.

Over the course of that week, an estimated 125,000 visitors came to the Abbey. The week ended with the Pontifical Mass celebrated by Archbishop Schulte of Indianapolis, who bestowed the Pope's Apostolic Blessing on all who came. The abovementioned writer who compared the event to the 1939

World's Fair recounted the final blessing of the event, not without a noticeable tinge of nostalgia:

> Although "Fatima Week" has come to a close, its spiritual impact will be felt throughout the world for many years to come. There can be no doubt that the countless prayers and sacrifices offered during that time were most pleasing to Almighty God and His Blessed Mother. And Mary, through the goodness and mercy of Her Immaculate Heart, has sanctioned the paternal Apostolic Blessing and pledge of the Holy Father.[141]

OUR LADY'S UNIVERSAL MISSION

As Mother of the universal Church, Our Lady's mission is international in every sense of the term. The Greek word "catholic" simply means "universal." Nowhere is the catholicity of Her love more evident or Catholic than in Our Lady's various apparitions (to people of all races, languages and times) and in the missionary journeys of the Pilgrim Virgin Statue. At the risk of inundating the reader with historical details, it is my hope to paint a vivid picture of Our Lady's global mission by means of the Pilgrim Virgin Statue and the way in which She plants seeds of the Gospel among people of all races, cultures, and even religions. Other books may address the theological differences between Catholics and these other religions – a worthy subject in its own right – but that is not our purpose here. For the moment, I only wish to show how Our Lady *sees every single person on the face of the earth* as Her own beloved child. A systematic view of Her global outreach will help us to form a clearer picture of Her universal apostolate of faith. Since I have focused so much on North American and European stories up to this point in the book, I will limit the rest of this chapter to the three other large regions of the world where the Pilgrim Virgin has brought blessings and consolations. Asia, Africa, and Latin America.

Asia and Oceania:
These regions that host half the world's population may be the most fruitful of all Our Lady's mission fields. Ironically, they are also the least Christian areas

141   Ibid., 11.

of the world. We can only highlight some of the most extraordinary visitations of the Statue to nations in this part of the world, but the stories are inspiring:

- In Chapter 8 we spoke of the 1974 visit of the Statue to the war-torn country of Vietnam where the President of the Republic welcomed the Statue and two million people came out to pray with Our Lady.[142] This was a reprise of a visit of the Statue to that country in 1965, with similar crowds. As a result of that earlier visit, the Vietnamese had requested their own "National Pilgrim Virgin Statue" which inspired the effort to consecrate and crown replicas of the Pilgrim Virgin Statue simultaneously all throughout the world in 1971.[143]

- Catholic Philippines, of course, has always produced the greatest crowds to welcome Our Lady's Statue, particularly in the 1980s when the political situation was so desperate. In 1984 John Haffert brought a "World Peace Flight" to the Philippines and 60,000 people greeted the pilgrims' plane at the airport. At an outdoor Mass in Luneta Park in Manila, presided over by His Eminence, Jaime Cardinal Sin, an estimated crowd of two million pilgrims attended.[144] The following year, the good people of the Philippines did it again. Another crowd of over two million people showed up to greet the Pilgrim Virgin Statue when She was present at the closing of the Marian Year. At that time, Cardinal Sin stated that "it is indeed of great significance that the International Pilgrim Virgin Statue comes to our country … as we go through our darkest hour."[145] The Cardinal's "darkest hour" reference is to the troubled days of the waning Ferdinand Marcos dictatorship in the Philippines. The Statue returned to the Philippines in 1996 to a similar reception (though no statistics were kept) and received a new crown on May 13th, the anniversary of the first apparition at Fatima. John Haffert called that event "the single greatest demonstration in honor

142   *Soul* Magazine, March-April, 1975.

143   Haffert, *Dear Bishop*, 255.

144   Joseph F.S. Blahut, "The Philippine 'Miracle'", *Soul* Magazine, July-August, 1986.

145   Kaczmarek, *Wonders She Performs*, 158.

of Our Lady *ever* to have taken place in history."[146]

- The vast subcontinent of India is home to a sixth of the world's population and has hosted the Pilgrim Virgin Statue numerous times. Each time Our Lady goes there the response of people of all faiths is incredible. The Pilgrim Virgin visited various sites of faith in India during the 1978 World Peace Flight, and while the Statue was in Bombay at least one million people came to see Her.[147] In a three-month tour through the region of Kerala, India in 2003-04 as many as *four million* people of all faiths flocked to see the Statue. Numerous documented healings and miracles were attributed to the visit of the Pilgrim Virgin Statue.[148]

- In addition to those mentioned above, the Statue has visited many other countries of Asia and Oceania: Australia, China, Cambodia, South Korea, Singapore, Indonesia, Hong Kong, Tahiti, Guam, Fiji, Saipan / Commonwealth of the Northern Mariana Islands (CNMI), Japan, Sri Lanka, and Thailand, among others. The Statue has visited many of these countries multiple times in Her seventy years of mission.

Africa:
The Pilgrim Virgin Statue has graced the immense continent of Africa with Her presence a number of times and always with the most enthusiastic responses by the people. It is difficult to glean accurate crowd statistics about the trips to Africa from the various publications describing them, so I will offer here a few simple descriptions of the many visits that Our Lady's Statue has made to Africa.

- Africa was one of the first continents to receive Our Lady's embrace; the Statue made a trip to Africa as early as 1949,[149] which touched upon the highly diverse countries of Morocco in the North; Uganda, Ethiopia, and Kenya in the East; Angola in the West; Tanzania, Zanzibar,

---

146   John M. Haffert, *The Day I Didn't Die* (Asbury, NJ: LAF, 1998), 37.

147   Kaczmarek, *Wonders She Performs*, 45.

148   Carl Malburg, *The Fatima Times* Newsletter, May 2008. Cf. also *IPVS News*, Fall 2012.

149   Haffert, *Russia Converted*, 216-17.

and Mozambique in the Southeast; South Africa and Rhodesia (later re-named Zimbabwe) in the South. A White Father missionary priest reported that at least 10,000 to 15,000 people turned up to greet the Pilgrim Virgin Statue at each venue. The crowds were of such diverse religious affiliations as Catholics, Anglicans, Muslims, Hindus, and animists, all of whom venerated Our Lady together. The crowds were equally diverse in racial mixture, which was something of a miracle in itself. He noted that "to the great astonishment of ...the press, 20,000 people, Blacks, Indians, and Whites knelt side by side at an outdoor midnight Mass in Johannesburg. Such a demonstration was deemed impossible."[150] But of course Our Lady made it possible.

• Following Pope Paul VI's visit to the Shrine of Fatima for the Golden Jubilee of the apparitions (May 13th, 1967), a World Peace Flight went on what John Haffert called a "circle tour" of the African continent. He noted that the highlight of the trip was the reception in Uganda where crowds lined the road for miles to get a glimpse of the Pilgrim Virgin Statue.[151]

• On that trip the Statue visited the countries of Ethiopia, Morocco, Zanzibar (largely Muslim), Tanzania, and Mozambique; the Statue also went to South Africa as part of the 1983 World Peace Flight.

Latin America:
Perhaps nowhere in the world is the soil for the Gospel message as fertile as in the truly Catholic continent of Latin America, the land which Pope John Paul II named "the continent of hope." With minor interruptions, pilgrimages throughout South America extended from 1974 until 1982 under the custodianship of the Society for the Defense of Tradition, Family and Property (TFP) while the founder Dr. Plinio Corrêa de Oliveira was still alive. It is significant to note that during the 1970's, 1980's and 1990's, airlines in Latin America almost always treated the International Pilgrim Virgin Statue as a passenger, giving Her a free seat, with passengers and crewmembers alike treating Her with the utmost respect. The pious laity would often show their veneration and affec-

150   Ibid.
151   Haffert, *Dear Bishop*, 248-49.

tion for Our Lady openly whenever the Statue would pass by.

On one of my trips I remember clearly one lady kneeling before the Statue in studious attention for a good deal of time right in the airplane's central aisle prior to take-off. Like the African trips, we are not always able to piece together accurate statistics about crowd sizes and venues from the existing literature, but our purpose is mainly to paint a picture of how Our Lady receives such veneration and love when She goes about planting the seeds of the Gospel message in the fertile soil of the hearts of the faithful in Latin America.

- The Statue's 1976 pilgrimage, for example, witnessed an explosion of piety by people from all walks of life in various cities in Argentina, Brazil, Chile, Colombia, Ecuador, and Venezuela. In Caracas, Venezuela, for example, the Statue was visited by more than 60,000 faithful in a single day at the home of one of its more prominent citizens. An endless queue of devotees circled several blocks, waiting for hours on end to see the Statue of the Queen of Heaven and Earth up close, even if for just a brief moment. In Merida, Venezuela, a city of 80,000 inhabitants, the Statue was visited by some 11,000 people in one day (more than one-eighth of the population). In Medellin, Colombia, about 20,000 faithful streamed through the house where the Statue was being hosted, while in Mendoza, Argentina, 2,000 cadets paraded before the Statue giving it military honors.

- In the Statue's 1984 visit to Guayaquil, Ecuador, Archbishop Bernardino Echeverría (later named cardinal) was so overwhelmed by the turnout of the people to greet Our Lady that he said it was the greatest manifestation of religious fervor that he had seen in his entire life. In three days over 300,000 people made a visit to the Cathedral to see the Pilgrim Virgin Statue.

- In December of 2000, the Pilgrim Virgin Statue of Our Lady of Fatima visited seven parishes in the western section of the vast province of La Rioja, Argentina.[152] In the space of three weeks She imbued the people

---

152   "Peregrinación triunfal de la Sagrada Imagen por las montañas riojanas", *Relatorio del Viaje de la Sagrada Imagen al Oeste Riojano*, 11/27-12/18/00.

of that region with profound religious sentiments and extraordinary zeal. In one village, She was publicly proclaimed by the mayor as the "Most Illustrious Visitor" ever to enter their village and was given military honors. In another, the people put on a welcoming parade befitting a national hero. In yet another, virtually the entire village of 2,000 people came to see the Statue off and formed a caravan of eighty cars to take Her to the next village. In all, the Statue traversed some fifty cities, towns and villages of the region inspiring the local people to pray deeply, to love Christ and the Church more fervently, and to offer their sacrifices in reparation for the sins of humanity.

"THE MOST SPECIAL PERSON WE'VE EVER FLOWN WITH"

I could multiply the stories of the marvels that surround the Statue everywhere but I believe the picture I have been trying to paint is well-presented by now. Allow me to conclude this chapter with a personal account of how easily Our Lady can transform the hearts of people who are open to Her message. On a return trip from a pilgrimage to Brazil in 1999 I was checking in at the São Paulo-Guarulhos International Airport for my flight back to the United States. The Pilgrim Virgin was arriving in the terminal in a huge procession with hundreds of people praying and singing hymns. I noticed that the flight manager was monitoring the check ins and I asked her if the Statue could be upgraded to First Class, which sometimes happens when I fly in Latin American countries due to their deep love of the Blessed Virgin. She looked at me in surprise and with a smirk on her face said "I don't think so."

Interestingly, one of the ladies working at the counter recognized me from a previous trip, and said; "Hey, you're the one with the Statue, right? The one from last time?" I acknowledged that I was, and she commented with some humor in her voice, "Well, when you were here last year, you ran out of pictures and you owe me a picture!" I said, "Oh, I'm sorry. Ok." I then opened my briefcase and pulled out some pictures to give her. I always carry pictures and holy cards with me, as do all of the custodians, because people frequently ask for them. As I gave her one, all the other workers saw the exchange and asked for their own holy cards, which I willingly gave them. All this was observed by the manager. Upon finishing the check-in, the manager who had originally denied my request for an upgrade and had indicated that it was pretty far-fetched for me to have even brought it up, returned and said to me in a kidding way with a half-smile on her face, "Well, maybe there's a chance I could upgrade the Statue, but not you." I said, "Fine. That's what I wanted. I like to see the Statue in First Class." So she said, "Well, we'll see." Much to my surprise, when I got on the plane, both the Statue and I were escorted to the Business Class cabin of the Boeing 777 aircraft, which we had entirely to ourselves.

During take-off, word of the Statue got around to the crew, and during the initial ascent one-by-one, every crew member came to get a better look at Her. At one point the crew members were sitting down in the seats next to the Statue, asking me questions about Fatima, the Statue, and the crisis in the world, etc. I was very touched by their interest and delighted to minister to them in this way because the experience, once again, showed the immense grace and attraction of the Statue. I marveled at what was happening and reflected to myself: Here I am at 35,000 feet, talking to the crew, giving a lecture about Fatima, all because of this wonderful Statue. The experience was very moving. The attendants were so caught up in this discussion for about ten minutes that they forgot about their duties. Eventually, one of them exclaimed; "We better get to our stations! We have things to do!" So they all got up and left.

A short time later the head flight attendant was asking me about the Statue, about Fatima and its history. It turned out that he was a Roman Catholic. He was very touched by the story and the Statue. Soon after that, he called all the attendants together in the galley and pulled the curtain shut and I perceived that they were discussing the Statue and me, so I got a little worried. I thought we were going to get moved back to the cabin section, but my apprehension of that meeting turned out to be wrong. A minute later, the head flight attendant opened the curtain and came directly over and squatted down in the aisle next to me, delicately, as if he were going to break some bad news. He said, "Mr. McKenna, we just had a pow-wow, all of us in the crew. We realize that this Statue is so important; that it is not just any statue. Although this section is closed for lack of clientele, we don't want you to be away from the Statue. So we would like to propose two options for you: either you can stay back here – even though no one is supposed to be here – or we could put you and the Statue up in First Class." I asked him: "What would you prefer? I don't want to cause any problems for you." but he responded, "No, either way is fine." So I said, "Let's go up there. That way you won't have to have an attendant come here just to attend to me."

Immediately the flight attendant escorted the Statue and me up to First Class, and during the rest of the long flight the crew continued to hover over us with questions and admiring looks. Some of the people in First Class also got up to see the Statue and asked for pictures and to have their pictures taken with her; it was quite moving to see that people were entirely taken by her beautiful countenance, which is probably the most miraculous aspect of the Statue. At a certain point, when it was dark, many people were trying to see the Statue, and I thought of a way to make the greatest impression on all of them at once. I asked the crew for a flashlight, and when we focused the beam on Her face like a spotlight in the middle of the darkened cabin, everyone let out a collective, "Oooohhh, wow!" It was so wonderful to see how impressed they were with Her enchanting gaze.

When we finally arrived at our destination the crew wanted more information and books about Fatima so I asked for a list of their names and addresses and told them that I would send them all printed materials and pictures when I got home. They also wanted to take a group picture, which we arranged in the First Class cabin, and I sent the crew members a copy of that picture too. Each of them thanked me profoundly for the grace-filled opportunity to be there with the Statue. Most of the crew members were Catholic, but several were not, yet, the veneration that they all showed on the flight was heartfelt and deeply moving.

As I departed with the Pilgrim Virgin Statue, one of them came to me with a look of utter sincerity and said, "We've had movie stars, millionaires, we've had all kinds of celebrities on this airplane, but this is undoubtedly the most special passenger we've ever flown with."

I couldn't have agreed more.

In and With Her Son's Church

*Priests must be pure, very pure. They should not
busy themselves with anything except what concerns the Church and
souls. The disobedience of priests and religious to their superiors
and to the Holy Father gravely displeases Our Lord.*
~*Words of Fatima seer St. Jacinta Marto before her death in 1920.*

The call to conversion is, as it were, the entryway to the full understanding of the message of salvation. Jesus' mission was not only to
take away our sins through His sacrificial death but in fact to *destroy
the very power of sin* over us. This is His most important work as Savior. In
the first epistle of John, the Beloved Disciple says, "Whoever sins belongs to
the devil, because the devil has sinned from the beginning. Indeed, the Son of
God was revealed to destroy the works of the devil" (1 Jn 3:8). His definitive
victory over sin and the devil happened once in history on the Hill of Cal-
vary, but He wills that that one-time event must be perpetuated throughout
history – and that is the mission of the Church.

The main truth in all of this is that Christ's Church is not a bystander
or a secondary player in our fight against sin. The Church is a necessary element and ally in this battle. In times of scandal and poor leadership we can
get so caught up in the sins and weaknesses of churchmen that we forget that
the Church is the Mystical Body of Christ, that Our Lord Himself promised
that He would remain with the Church "until the end of the age" (Mt 28:20)
and that the "gates of hell" (Mt 16:18) would never prevail against Her. And
while we must look realistically at the human failings of both clerics and laity,

we must never forget that the Church is essentially of divine origin and the sacrament of salvation established by Our Lord to carry on His saving work throughout human history.

Isn't it curious that every time Our Lady appears on earth it is always with a gesture of profound respect for and obedience to the authority of the Church? Our Lady believes in the spiritual power of Her Son's Church. There is no instance in any authentic Marian apparition at any time in history where Our Lady asks anyone to disobey the Church's hierarchy or to set up an alternative church. If anyone would have the power to persuade people to do that, it would be Her. Yet, fidelity to the Church is a hallmark of Our Lady's appearances and a significant test of an apparition's authenticity. Our Lady is Mother of the Church and Mother of the Clergy. She knows that Her message will have the greatest effect only if those to whom She appears remain firmly under the divine mantle of the Church.

RUSSIA'S MARIAN BISHOP

"In and with the Church" is undoubtedly Our Lady's motto, but let us not think of the Church in abstract terms. Our Lady's embrace of Her Son's Church seems to be bound up with the *churchmen* who are specially chosen to carry out Her plans. I realized this in October of 2007 when then-Custodian Carl Malburg and I traveled to Fatima with the Pilgrim Virgin Statue for the occasion of the 90th anniversary of the apparitions. As part of the program, we attended an International Congress organized by the Fatima Shrine entitled "Fatima for the 21st Century." Among the more than half-million people who gathered at Fatima for the Anniversary of the Miracle of the Sun was Archbishop Tadeusz Kondrusiewicz, the first Catholic bishop assigned to Russia in the post-Communist era. He was chosen to head the Administration for European Russia, one of two mission territories designated by the Vatican at that time for the vast country of Russia. He had been consecrated bishop by Pope St. John Paul II in the late Eighties for his native country of Belarus, but he was given this critical assignment for Russia after the dissolution of the Soviet Union.

Carl and I were honored to meet the illustrious Archbishop and attend an early morning Mass he celebrated in the Chapel of the Apparitions for a group of Russian pilgrims who were accompanying him. The previous day I had met with some of these pilgrims and offered to have the International Pilgrim Virgin Statue of Our Lady of Fatima present for Mass. Archbishop Kondrusiewicz was very pleased with the idea because he fondly remembered the Statue's visit to his diocese in October of 1992 when the Statue was brought on pilgrimage to Red Square in Moscow. That day more than a thousand people had gathered in front of the Kremlin together with the Archbishop and the Orthodox Patriarch for the crowning of the Statue, together with the secret Russian statue that had been "hidden" in Moscow since 1950.

When the Archbishop learned that the Statue had arrived for the Mass that morning, he asked that She be placed in a prominent place on a pillar in front of the altar, which is very near where Our Lady had actually appeared in 1917. Upon entering the sanctuary he once again crowned Our Blessed Mother in a moving act of piety. Here, fifteen years later, he once again found himself in the presence of the same miraculous Statue in the very place where Our Lady had actually made that promise. I was very honored to carry the crown of Our Lady in the procession and present it to the Archbishop for the act of crowning.

During his sermon, the Archbishop spoke of his absolute faith and trust in Mary's promise for the conversion of Russia and of his own devotion to Our Lady of Fatima. At one point in the sermon, the Archbishop choked up with tears as he spoke fervently about Our Lady's promise for his country. In the presence of all, the Archbishop publicly thanked Our Lady for the gift of freedom in Russia. It was an immensely touching and significant moment for all who were in attendance, and indeed for all who believe in the message of Our Lady of Fatima.

I must say that a wave of nostalgia washed over me at the Mass when it occurred to me that this was the exact place where, *sixty years earlier,* the International Pilgrim Virgin Statue had first been blessed by the Bishop of Leiria-Fatima, together with the statue destined for Russia. Now the primary archbishop of Russia was crowning Her! Our Lady's pilgrimage *started here.* As if a symbol of faith's goal, Her image had come back "home," back to its very point of origin to remind us of what the pilgrimage of faith is all about: to bring us to our true home in Heaven.

The Pilgrim Virgin Statue Blesses San Diego

I had direct confirmation of Our Lady's union with the Church when I decided to move back to California in 2005. Prior to that I had spent twenty-four years living and working on the East Coast. For most of my life I had worked with the American Society for the Defense of Tradition, Family and Property (TFP) and its America Needs Fatima campaign. When I resigned from the organization and moved to San Diego I had no local network or resources aside from a friend in Auxiliary Bishop Salvatore Cordileone. I did not have any working relationships, but I had aspirations to create a dynamic organization that would have a positive impact on the mission of the Church.

At the time I consulted with my longtime friend with whom I have collaborated for over twenty years, Cardinal Raymond Burke. I discussed with him my ideas and that I wanted to found an organization to support and defend the principles of the Catholic Church. I decided to call the organization "Catholic Action for Faith and Family." Cardinal Burke was very encouraging and promised to support my efforts in any way he could. I have been very blessed with this relationship and we have continued to assist each other mutually until today.

But while great ideas are easy to come by, the many problems of a start-up organization immediately confronted me. I wanted to begin a Catholic apostolate in San Diego, but I knew literally no one but my wife Bridgette since I had recently relocated. Furthermore, as far as I could see, the Fatima movement in San Diego was somewhat defunct; no one was promoting Our Lady's message in any big way. I found out that in years past there had been a chapter of the Blue Army but that it had disbanded as most of the members gradually grew older. Worst of all, the local diocese had some months earlier announced the biggest pay-out of any diocese in history, up to that time, in compensation for the clergy sex abuse scandals. The local Catholic populace was naturally upset and demoralized by the news and by the consequences of the financial burden. I confess that I was not even aware of the extent of the scandals or the demoralization when I arrived in California, but that made my situation all the more challenging.

Yet, when I needed help the most, not surprisingly, I found it once again in the Pilgrim Virgin Statue of Our Lady of Fatima.

When I moved back to California in 2005 Mrs. Haffert had contacted me to ask if I would help her wrap up some of the lingering affairs of her late husband, the beloved John Haffert, the man who had brought the Pilgrim Virgin Statue into the world. Among other things, she asked if I would join the board of directors of the organization that conducted the programs with the Pilgrim Virgin Statue. Although I had collaborated and worked for years with the directors and the Hafferts in the travels and promotions of the Statue's activities, I had never served as a director. I was very honored and pleased and immediately agreed to her offer. Since I had time on my hands, it occurred to me that the Pilgrim Virgin Statue would be the most potent force possible to inaugurate the new outreach I was undertaking and further the apostolate of the Pilgrim Virgin. If it can be said, I made a *deal* with Our Lady to bring the Pilgrim Virgin Statue to San Diego for a mission trip as a means of great spiritual benefit to the Catholics of southern California. And, as a secondary benefit I asked her to open doors and introduce me to people with whom I could begin collaborating if it was Her will. Never did I make a better *deal*.

PLANNING

I began to work on the new project which would develop over the next year. January of 2008 was available so I decided on that month. I have already spoken in previous chapters about Our Lady's ability to open doors and hearts, and She did exactly that as I was planning the first big event for Catholic Action for Faith and Family.

Where was I to begin such a huge undertaking? I first contacted a woman who had befriended me some months earlier following a Sunday Mass at a church in down town San Diego. She had noticed me and came over to talk. Her name was Sue Lopez and she was a dedicated pro-life advocate who had formed a dynamic local chapter of Helpers of God's Precious Infants founded by Msgr. Philip Reilly in New York. Every Saturday she faithfully led a group of sidewalk counselors to pray at abortion clinics and to dissuade women from having abortions. She took great interest in this project and offered to help coordinate it. She also introduced me to Kent Peters, the director of the Office of Social Ministry of the Diocese of San Diego, who obtained permission of the diocesan bishop to conduct the pilgrimage. This allowed me to begin contacting and visiting parishes of the diocese asking for their participation in the upcoming event. I had a three week tour planned for the Pilgrim Virgin Statue, and my goal was to have Her visit a parish a day as is customary

Since the visit would coincide with the infamous anniversary of the Supreme Court decision, *Roe v. Wade,* that legalized abortion in our country in 1973, we planned to make a pro-life march the centerpiece of Our Lady's visit to San Diego because I believed She wanted that and that She would bring such an event to fruition like never before. The Bishop gave his blessing but offered no tangible help in promoting the event other than granting approval. Parish commitments seemed to trickle in for many months, not in the way I had hoped or needed. This was set to be the biggest tour of any kind in the history of the Diocese of San Diego, but the progress was slow as the deadline approached. Numerous times during the months of preparation I asked myself, "Am I really going to be able to fill three weeks' worth of parish visits?" As the time for the event drew closer, the parish visitation calendar still had many vacancies. I redoubled my prayers and retreated to my motto and my deepest belief in Our Lady's assistance, "With Our Lady everything always works out well in the end."

As I mentioned before, the local pro-life community, particularly the Helpers of God's Precious Infants, were enthusiastic backers of the event, not only in helping to spread news about it but also in offering much-needed spiritual support without which something of this magnitude could not be a success. In the early stages of the planning I contacted San Diego's then-Auxiliary Bishop, now Archbishop, Salvatore Cordileone, who was undoubtedly the greatest and most public supporter of the event. He gave us permission to hold a pro-life prayer vigil in the Cathedral on the Sunday afternoon of the event and promised to be the main celebrant of the prayer service and the keynote speaker of the prayer march to follow.

THE MOMENTUM GROWS

As January approached, it seemed that the days sped up. I put in long hours trying to organize the final details, and there were quite a few open parish slots left, even up to the last few weeks. Yet, I continued to entrust the whole event to Her. Somewhere in the final push I was contacted by a good Marian friend and colleague that John Haffert had introduced me to many years before, Mr. Bud McFarlane, who informed me that his daughter lived in San Diego and that – providentially – her husband, Steve Breen, was a Pulitzer Prize-winning cartoonist for the local newspaper. Bud connected me with Steve, and my new inside contact for the San Diego *Union Tribune* was instrumental in gaining us a significant amount of unexpected pre-event publicity. Steve said he really didn't know how to pitch an event with a religious theme to the paper so I suggested using a 2004 front page article in the *Chicago Tribune* about the Pilgrim Virgin Statue as evidence of the public's interest and prestige. Steve was then able to present the idea of the Pilgrim Virgin's visit to the local religion editor, who, much to our surprise, decided to cover it.

Not only did the editor cover the event, but she did so in a professional and friendly manner, which had not always been the tone of the religion section of that paper toward Catholicism especially in light of the sex abuses crisis. Nonetheless, all these amazing connections, even at the last minute, seemed to point to Our Lady's work behind the scenes publicizing Her own event, and the incredible un-earned publicity portended well for what was to come. Not only did the religion editor interview me before the event, but she provided substantial coverage of it in the religion section of the paper and even gave the full day-by-day itinerary of the Statue's entire three-week visit, a lavish favor which rarely occurs. It was the best possible promotion we could have wished for. The same writer even did a lengthy follow-up story mid-way through the pilgrimage. When Kent Peters saw that we got two extensive publicity articles in the *Union Tribune*, itinerary included, he was very surprised. He asked me how I had done this, and I told him that it was Our Lady's influence, not mine. Never had so much positive publicity been given to anything Catholic in several years.

An additional stressor for me immediately prior to the Statue's arrival was the illness of my father who had to come to San Diego unexpectedly for quintuple bypass surgery. I cannot put into words how difficult it was for me to balance the myriad details of the preparations for the tour with concern for my father's wellbeing. Two priest friends were also in town for a visit with me that had been planned the year before. All these important obligations converged on me at the same time, and I kept telling myself, "Confide! *Confide!* Have confidence in Our Lady's power to pull this off."

AN OVERFLOW OF GRACE AND FAVOR

The Statue arrived in San Diego in early January of 2008 and I can say with absolute candor that the three week tour was an utterly amazing outpouring of grace. Attendance was unprecedented: at every parish there were out-the-door crowds, packed liturgies, and, most importantly, priests overwhelmed by the number of confessions they had to hear. Those priests who might have been skeptical of a simple Statue prior to the visit ended up impressed during those weeks. In fact, in the build-up to the event, when the Marian fervor was at its peak, we couldn't accommodate all the requests of the priests who wanted the Statue to visit their parish. How foolish of me to worry about filling all the slots for parish visitations. My anxieties were gone by the time the Statue arrived. We actually had the opposite problem on our hands: we were obliged to extend the tour for two or three extra days in order to fulfill all the demands for the Statue, and even then we could not accommodate all the requests.

Carl Malburg, then-custodian of the Statue, was truly impressed at the turn-out in San Diego. He told me that normally when he traveled with the Statue he would bring a significant cache of materials to sell and distribute during a tour, but he quickly expended all his stocks in San Diego and had to ask his dedicated wife Rose Mary to send more materials to meet the demand during the three weeks. In fact, he thought he had ordered more than he needed and expected to take home what was not used. However, he had to reorder materials several times during those weeks and each time he did, the materials evaporated faster than he had ever seen. The distribution rate for everything from literature to religious articles (as well as a windfall of donations) took place at triple the normal rate of most diocesan tours with the Statue. A total of 26,000 scapulars were distributed during the pilgrimage and an immense amount of literature and holy images. Many of those who received the scapulars also participated in the scapular enrollment ceremonies. Mr. Malburg also estimates that 954 books, 28,300 booklets in English, 5,800 booklets in Spanish, as well as 6,400 large pictures and 8,000 small pictures were distributed in that three week period.

As is evident, the response of the people to the visit of the Pilgrim Virgin Statue was simply overwhelming. Carl commented to me that in his twenty-five years of accompanying the Statue, he had never seen a venue in the US as successful for teaching and evangelizing as the Diocese of San Diego. They estimated that somewhere between 50,000 and 60,000 people attended and participated in the pilgrimage at the various parishes during those weeks. This was an immense blessing for the diocese.

It would not be an overstatement to say that the three-week visit of the Pilgrim Virgin Statue to San Diego rallied the diocese and was a perfectly-timed force of spiritual consolation for many faithful who had been so beleaguered by news of the scandals. Many of the priests and laity came to the same conclusion and commented about this to me. I could not lay claim to even one ounce of the credit for Our Lady's perfect timing. I had no clue that things would turn out as well as they did. I was just one of the many workers who helped Our Queen carry off an event of such grace and favor that people could not believe what they were experiencing. Our Lady's visit seemed to produce a cascade of grace and favor for the faithful in San Diego.

A TRUE GLORY FOR OUR LADY

Sunday, January 20th marked the high point of Our Lady's visit: the March for the Unborn in anticipation of the anniversary of *Roe v. Wade*. At the conclusion of the event we sent out a press release that highlighted all the details of the event.[153] The statement speaks for itself:

On Sunday, January 20, more than seven hundred faithful gathered in

---

153   "Catholics Fill San Diego Cathedral and Process Through the Streets to Decry 35 Years of Legalized Abortion in the US," Press Release of Catholic Action for Faith and Family, 1/21/07.

San Diego's St. Joseph's Cathedral for prayer and a procession to decry thirty-five years of legalized abortion in the United States. The procession was led by auxiliary bishop, Salvatore Cordileone, and was blessed with the presence of the International Pilgrim Virgin Statue of Our Lady of Fatima.

Thomas McKenna, president of Catholic Action for Faith and Family, organized the event. He called it a *"Procession of Reparation"* to decry the January 22nd anniversary of the 1973 Supreme Court decision legalizing abortion in the United States. McKenna said that the infamous anniversary coincided with the three-week tour of the statue he had organized for the diocese in January, so he tied the two together. "In the past thirty-five years more than forty-eight million children have been killed in their mother's womb, and the message Our Lady gave at Fatima in 1917 spoke of this type of extreme moral decay," he said. "At Fatima the Blessed Mother asked for prayer and reparation, and that is what we did."

People gathered in the cathedral where the Fatima Statue was displayed. As the choir intoned hymns, the faithful filed out onto the street. Some of the participants stayed in the cathedral in adoration before the Blessed Sacrament which was exposed after people left.

The procession stretched over three city blocks as the people prayed the rosary in unison and chanted hymns. A police escort stopped traffic at intersections as the faithful walked just over a mile to the Family Planning Associates Abortion Center located across the street from San Diego's Balboa Park. At the park participants gathered on the lawn across the street from the clinic for a brief address by Bishop Cordileone and Mr. Kent Peters, the director of the diocesan Office for Social Ministry. After a solemn blessing by the bishop, the procession returned to the cathedral along the same route.

"It is not every day you see a liturgically-vested bishop, with miter and crosier leading hundreds of the faithful in procession through the streets of a major American city," commented Sue Lopez of Helpers of God's Precious Infants who leads weekly prayer vigils at the clinic. She said "it was very inspiring, a day to be remembered." The presence of many religious in their habits added to the solemnity of the day.

Upon arriving at the cathedral, the group filled the pews and sang the Salve Regina as the statue entered the church led by the bishop and a color guard escort from the Knights of Columbus. With Our Lady beside the altar and the Blessed Sacrament exposed in the monstrance, the bishop delivered a very inspiring meditation followed by Benediction.

As the bishop processed out giving his apostolic blessing, the church was filled with voices singing Holy God We Praise Thy Name and tears could be seen in the eyes of many.

THE EUCHARISTIC DIMENSION OF FATIMA

In studying the apparitions of Fatima, it was a revelation to me to learn that the day on which Our Lady appeared to the three shepherd children in 1917 was the feast day of *Our Lady of the Blessed Sacrament* in Portugal. Her visit had been prepared the year before by the Angel who brought the Eucharist to the children and taught them to worship Jesus in the Blessed Sacrament. We must not miss the profound significance of this connection of Fatima with the Eucharist.

Our Lady desires to unite us under the banner of the Eucharistic Christ and immerse us more deeply into the very lifeblood of the Church when we worship Him in the most Holy Sacrament of the altar. The pro-life prayer march in San Diego was none other than an immense act of Eucharistic reparation for souls in which adoration of the Blessed Sacrament was the key spiritual force behind the power of the march. There are many reasons why Our Lady wishes us to remain united to the Church, but I am convinced that the primary reason is *Eucharistic*: the Church is the one custodian of this greatest mystery of our Faith for all humanity. This Sacrament is the font of reparation and redemption.[154]

Our final event at the Cathedral was also a monumental step forward for the pro-life movement and brought hundreds of people into the effort to make reparation for the heinous crime of abortion, the defining issue of our day. It is astounding to think that Our Lady of Fatima understood, a full cen-

154   Johnston, *Great Sign,* 93-94.

tury ago, that one of the spiritual evils that would spread like a cancer from the systematic atheism of Russia was the abortion demon. Abortion is one of the worst "errors of Russia" that Our Lady warned the world about back in 1917. The world didn't listen then, but She does not cease to be a witness to that truth even now.

IT IS OUR LADY'S CHURCH

The other truth that profoundly impressed me about the event was that Our Lady does Her best work in and through the Church. She doesn't work *around* the Church (by which I mean Church authority); She works *in and through* the Church, and that is precisely the reason why She is so spiritually powerful in all that She does. Her attitude of submission to authority and humility makes all the difference in a largely Protestant country where people find it so easy to stand on their own authority for every question of religion and morality. While Our Lady radiates immense authority by Her holiness, She is also humble and will never undermine the spiritual authority structure of the Church established by Her Son. We tend to view the failings of churchmen as a weakness of our Church, but Our Lady does not. She sees these as an opportunity to teach us to have a greater degree of trust in the power of the Holy Spirit operating in and through the Church for the salvation of souls. She gave Our Lord His human body; but She is also a member of His Mystical Body with us and shows us how important it is to remain obedient to the Church in all things. It is within the Church that we accomplish the greatest spiritual works of prayer and atonement, and that solid spiritual principle was entirely evident in San Diego during those three blessed weeks.

Yet, the Custodians and organizers of the Pilgrim Virgin Statue have followed this principle of religious obedience from the very beginning of the Statue's travels to this day. In fact, the second Bishop of Leiria-Fatima, Most Rev. John Venancio, used to offer a fervent word of encouragement to the members of the Blue Army and to those who accompanied the Statue. He often exhorted them to "[a]lways obey the Bishop, and if he says no, do what is permitted, and quietly persist, quietly continue to knock as Our Lord commanded." John Haffert added that

[s]ometimes the Voice of God says "no" because there has been insufficient preparation, insufficient selflessness and humility, perhaps insufficient prayer and sacrifice – without which no seeds of the Apostolate would take root. But what bishop in the world would say "no" to an apostolate of holiness in his diocese if he were convinced that those promoting it were sincere and that the Apostolate was a sound one..... [The Blue Army] Apostolate has been built upon this awareness of the authority of the bishop and his role as the Voice of God.[155]

John Haffert certainly followed this advice strictly. As we noted earlier, he was refused permission by Cardinal Spellman to bring the Statue into New York on its inaugural journey to North America in October of 1947, and he respectfully obeyed the Cardinal's wishes. Instead, he accepted the invitation of several other bishops in Canada and went there first. Eventually the Statue was invited to the US through other friendly bishops and ultimately found its way back to the Archdiocese of New York. From its beginning to this day the Statue will only go officially to a diocese where the local bishop has given permission. It is my certain conviction that this is the real reason why the Statue brings so much grace and favor wherever She goes. She stays perfectly united with her Son's Church, of which She is the greatest symbol and representative.

In the End, Our Lady will Triumph

Businessmen talk often about win-win negotiations where two parties in a business deal work out the details of the matter to their mutual advantage. Well, in Our Lady's San Diego visit, it seemed that *everybody* won. A couple of weeks after the excitement had wound down and the wrap-up was finished, I distinctly recall reflecting on the visit and the fruits it had obtained. At that same moment, however, I marveled at how Our Lady had answered my prayer with a series of spiritual benefits that resonated in the hearts of faithful believers in the Diocese of San Diego, from the bishop to the hum-

155   Haffert, *Dear Bishop*, 152.

blest pro-life counselor on the street. As someone new to the diocese, I hadn't lived through their trauma brought about by the clergy scandal, but I had contributed something to the local church that had greatly exceeded my original intentions. Many people as well as clergy told me that they took Our Lady's visit as a sign of hope.

For my part, months before, when I made my *deal* with Our Lady, I was at the beginning of my new mission. I needed Our Lady to open a few doors for me, and the Pilgrim Virgin was the one I knew who could best accomplish that task. A little over one year later, the truth of Her answer to my prayer was very clear: the local bishops now knew us, the clergy, the pro-life movement, many religious orders, and a good section of the faithful now knew of Catholic Action for Faith and Family. In the end, scores of doors and relationships were opened for me and even more hearts were opened to the message that was central to our apostolate.

I'm happy to report that my Dad eventually recovered from his quintuple bypass surgery and returned to full health. The man who had taught me about Our Lady was in very good hands, and our family has had him back whole and sound for many years.

More importantly, Our Lady had breathed a breath of fresh air and inspiration into Her Son's Church, and we were all the better for it. In our most prayerful moments, faithful in San Diego could say, "Look! Look at what Our Lady did!"

IN THE END,
MY IMMACULATE HEART WILL TRIUMPH

*May the message of Fatima be increasingly accepted, understood and
lived in every community. Although anxieties and sufferings have not been
lacking, and there are still reasons for apprehension about the future of
humanity, what the "Lady in white" promised to the little shepherds
is consoling: "In the end, my Immaculate Heart will triumph."*
~Pope Benedict XVI, message for the 25th anniversary of the
assassination attempt on John Paul II, May 13th, 2006.

Our sad world is awash with terrorist acts, which seem to be increasing daily.
As the percentage of people with an active Christian faith drops, religious
persecution rises, heinous crimes and monstrous new forces of destruction
are unleashed against the most vulnerable citizens of our world, and our religious and political leaders seem powerless to stop them. Waves of evil continually wash over our societies, and we have to ask: *Where* is the promised
Triumph of Our Lady's Immaculate Heart? A full century after She promised
the victory of Her Heart over evil, we are still awaiting it.

One thing is clear from the start: the seeming absence or delay of the
Triumph of Her Heart is not at all Our Lady's fault. Our Lady was meticulous
in Her wording when She noted that Her victory would only come "in the end."
There is a coherent message in that specific wording. We may well imagine that
Our Lady knew Her message would be spurned, ignored and mocked, or perhaps even heeded by some but with incomplete zeal for the seriousness of Her
words. Like the Parable of the Sower in the Gospel (cf. Mt 13:1-9), some would
ignore the words of the message to the extent that the servants of Satan would
come and snatch them from their hearts like seeds taken off the hard path by

the birds of the air. Others would welcome them with superficial enthusiasm bearing little or no fruit, while still others would have the message choked out of their souls by the many cares and addictions of a tainted world.

THE LAST AND MOST TRAGIC KING OF FRANCE

History bears witness that there is a price to pay for failing to heed a divine invitation. Just like the people in the Gospel who were summoned to the wedding feast but turned down the offer for various reasons (cf. Mt 22:1-14), so we can miss or overlook our opportunity to be part of Her victory if we do not conform ourselves to Her simple plan. There is a heartbreaking story about King Louis XIV of France who was instructed by Our Lord through an apparition given to St. Margaret Mary Alocoque that he should consecrate France to the Sacred Heart and emblazon the Heart of Jesus on his country's flag and coat of arms. In so doing, the king would receive a life of grace and eternal glory, as well as victory over his enemies. The date of the apparition was June 17th, 1689.[156]

The famous "Sun King" either refused or *neglected* to carry out Our Lord's wishes at that time. His successor, Louis XV, did not perform the consecration either. Two royal generations later, in the firestorm of evil leading up to the French Revolution, King Louis XVI had still not performed the consecration. The king was deprived of royal dignity and power on June 17th, 1789, exactly one hundred years *to the day* of the message that was given to his grandfather by the Sacred Heart. But the story doesn't end there.

As of 1792, after Louis XVI had been imprisoned in the Tower of the Temple, this request had still not been heeded. The king then made the vow to consecrate himself, his family, and his kingdom to the Sacred Heart of Jesus if he regained his freedom, the crown, and royal power. It was too late: the king left prison only for his execution.[157]

---

156   Fr Richard Heilman, "Our Lady of Fatima, 1917-2017 – Why 100 Years Matters," Roman Catholic Man, 2/01/16; http://www.romancatholicman.com/our-lady-of-fatima-1917-2017-why-100-years-matters/.

157   Antonio A. Borelli, *Fatima: Past or Future? The Unheeded Message*, Glasgow: Tradition, Family, Property, 2005, footnote, 106.

The failure of three generations of the Bourbon royal dynasty to fulfill God's Will in a timely manner may be one of the greatest missed opportunities of history.

Will we let the time of Our Lady's will for saving our world pass? Will we neglect the message? She certainly has done Her part and therefore so much depends upon *our* cooperation. While the hour is indeed late, I don't believe that we are too late to heed the message of Fatima. We haven't reached the end yet; we haven't seen Her definitive Triumph. I believe, rather, that there is a deeper reason for the delay. I share the sentiments of an Italian writer and commentator who declared that:

> [w]e are on the threshold of the Great Promise of Fatima, that of the Woman Clothed with the Sun, at the dawn of a new era of peace: She, who will triumph with a sudden mysterious act and will clothe humanity in a new light – the radiant light of the Immaculate Heart of Mary … who continuously prays, cries and suffers with [Her Son's] Church, for the loss of Her children, hoping to the very last for their salvation, as a mother does on the threshold of giving birth to new life.[158]

We have reason to hope for that imminent victory both because the Triumph of Her Heart is God's explicit Will and because the time of reckoning for the sins of the modern age seems to be rapidly approaching.

DEVOTION TO THE IMMACULATE HEART OF MARY IS GOD'S WILL

First of all, no serious student of the apparitions of Fatima can miss Our Lady's distinct references to the Will of God that are inserted into the heart of Her message. In fact, lack of reference to God's Will would have constituted a serious omission undermining the powerful impact of the message. The suggestion that the entire Fatima event was given to us *because God Himself*

---

158 Francesca Bonadonna, "Fatima: the prophecy of a crisis and the promise of an eagerly awaited triumph," *Rorate Caeli*, 5/13/16; translated and reprinted from the Italian publication, *Famiglia Domani*, 5/22/14; http://rorate-caeli.blogspot.com/2015/05/fatima-prophecy-of-crisis-and-promise.html.

willed it accomplishes several purposes: not only does it help us defend our Faith against any accusations of "Mariolatry" brought against us, but it also establishes Mary as a servant of His purposes and devotion to Her Immaculate Heart as His distinct desire for humanity's spiritual welfare. Our Lady told the children in the June 1917 apparition that "Jesus wants to use you to make me known and loved. He wishes to establish the devotion to My Immaculate Heart throughout the world." In effect, *Jesus Himself* wants us to be devoted to the Immaculate Heart of Mary.

The third apparition to the shepherd children was Our Lady's longest message, but as always She said nothing superfluous. July's message followed the horrific vision of Hell that gave the children a view of the grotesque reality from which Our Lady was trying to save us. It was then that Our Lady pronounced the words, "God wishes" for the second time: "To save [souls], God wishes to establish in the world devotion to my Immaculate Heart." This phrase, this message, this truth rests at the very heart of Her message in every sense of the word. A perceptive reader will note that the phrase ("God wishes", which reaffirms the June phrase, "Jesus...wishes") stands in the *exact center* of the six apparitions. If we exclude the more mundane exchanges between Our Lady and Lucia (requests for cures and other matters), there are approximately 890 words of strict dialogue in the English translation. The "God wishes" phrase occurs at the 442 word mark. This is the exact linguistic center of Her message.[159] That placement is not without meaning.

In other words, by establishing devotion to Our Lady's Immaculate Heart, Our Lord seeks to hasten the victory of Her Heart over the destructive forces of sin and Satan in the modern age. But we must understand this devotion correctly. Even fervent devotion to the Immaculate Heart does not guarantee that our lives will be free of suffering; it certainly didn't save the three shepherd children from their sometimes terrible sufferings. Rather, true devotion to the Immaculate Heart is a way of participating more deeply in the Cross of Christ and assisting Our Lady in atoning for the sins of our generation. It is sin that visits disaster upon us. The Immaculate Heart of Mary devotion is the antidote to the self-destructive direction of our world. She warned the world very clearly in the third apparition that "various nations will be annihilated." But the message of penitence is ongoing and grows more

159   In John Haffert's 1993 book, *Her Own Words.*

urgent each day with the increase of sin in the latter part of the 20th and early part of the 21st Centuries. We as the heirs of the Fatima message are not allowed to rest from praying for intercession.

A TIME OF RECKONING?

Another reason for our hope in the Triumph of Our Lady's Immaculate Heart is the understanding that a sufficient number of warnings have now been given. When the Vatican made known the content of the Third Secret of Fatima[160] in the year 2000, one of the elements that most surprised even the most avid Fatima-watchers was the vision of the fierce Angel with the flaming sword poised to strike humanity with God's retribution for sin:

> [A]t the left of Our Lady and a little above, we saw an Angel with a flaming sword in his left hand; flashing, it gave out flames that looked as though they would set the world on fire; but they died out in contact with the splendor that Our Lady radiated towards him from her right hand. pointing to the earth with his right hand, the Angel cried out in a loud voice: 'Penance, Penance, Penance!'

Perhaps this image should not have been surprising to anyone because the overall message of Fatima included a warning about the consequences of sin and a call to penance. Nevertheless, talk of a flaming sword ready to scorch the world in due justice for sin conveys a sense of doom that we are not accustomed to in the modern age. The image indicates the absolute consistency of the message of repentance for the past hundred years, however. It is an *urgent* message, a fervent call to conversion and penance for the entire human race, and its urgency has not diminished in a full century since Our Lady appeared.

It is not my intent to rehash the discussions and conflict surrounding the revelation of the Third Secret. That has been done by others. My concern is to point out that the "day of reckoning" inherent in the image of the Angel of Justice for the sins of the modern age is imminent but *has not yet arrived*. The image of the Angel with the fiery sword was only made known

160   Congregation for the Doctrine of the Faith, *The Message of Fatima*, 6/26/00.

to the world in the year 2000 constituting perhaps the last and most poignant Fatima warning to our generation. A reasonable person may ask whether our sinful world has any warnings left.

Mr. Haffert also thought that the apparitions of Our Lady of Akita in Japan in 1973 were an echo of the message of Fatima. The apparitions of Akita consisted of three messages given in 1973 to a Japanese nun, Sr. Agnes Sasagawa, together with the holy Stigmata in her hands and a miraculous cure from deafness some years later. The final message of Akita was given on October 13th, 1973, confirming in one of many ways the connection with Fatima. Akita's messages also included a distinct preparation of the seer by an angel, several requests to pray the Rosary for reparation, a statue that wept, and a message of urgent penance and conversion. The Akita messages received approval of the local bishop in 1984 after a lengthy investigation.

As the hundred-year delay of the kings of France to implement the desires of the Sacred Heart unleashed the satanic evil of the French Revolution, we may legitimately surmise that a hundred-year delay in the full implementation of Our Lady's plan for world peace weighs heavily upon humanity and has already allowed unprecedented evils to enter upon the modern age. In a 1982 letter to Pope John Paul II, Sr. Lucia commented that the threat of "annihilation" spoken about in the 1917 apparitions continues to hang over the human race and that "we are going toward it...with great strides."[161] In other words, the time of reckoning is in our hands and depends upon how we respond to Our Lady's plea for penance and conversion. The Fatima call to penance, prayer and conversion is more urgent than ever.

MARIAN FORMATION

Devotion to the Immaculate Heart of Mary is Our Lord's and Our Lady's response to God's demands of justice. This devotion requires us to form ourselves in Our Blessed Mother's virtues, habits, and even thought patterns; this is to say, we must be like a mass of clay in the hands of a master potter in order to become like Her. The clay is a humble substance, without clear

---

161   Sr. Lucia's handwritten letter to Pope John Paul II was cited in the Congregation for the Doctrine of the Faith, *The Message of Fatima*, Introduction, 6/26/00.

form or beauty, whose singular virtue rests in its malleability. In the hands of an accomplished artist, the amorphous clay is gradually transformed into a work of art or a vessel into which God's grace may be poured. That process of allowing ourselves to be molded and formed by Our Lady into a beautiful vessel is the process of interior formation in the Christian life. If we give ourselves over to Her through devotion to the Immaculate Heart, then our transformation is assured, and we become transformed – over time – into Her instruments for the salvation of the world.

We need have no fear that our affection for Our Lady will detract from our love of Jesus. That simply is not possible. It was clarified long ago by the great Marian saint, Louis Marie de Montfort, that consecration to Our Lady is in fact *the most direct pathway* to Christ:

> Our entire perfection consists in being conformed, united and consecrated to Jesus Christ. Hence the most perfect of all devotions is undoubtedly that which conforms, unites and consecrates us most perfectly to Jesus Christ. Now, since Mary is of all creatures the one most conformed to Jesus Christ, it follows that among all devotions that which most consecrates and conforms a soul to our Lord is devotion to Mary, his Holy Mother, and that the more a soul is consecrated to her the more will it be consecrated to Jesus Christ.[162]

In that regard, our interior transformation will only be complete when our hearts become like Hers; that is, when we adopt the intentions of Our Lady of Fatima as our primary concern.

Perhaps the best testimony to the power of this transformation is little Jacinta Marto, the youngest person ever to be canonized by our Church. She had not even reached her tenth birthday when she died. Yet, her two-and-a-half years of both voluntary and involuntary suffering after the apparitions would put the strongest saints to shame. Jacinta had so interiorized the intentions of Our Lady of Fatima that we can speak of her as literally having become one with Our Lady's will to save the world through penance. Jacinta died of the horrible disease of pleurisy after having suffered the extremely

---

162   Quoted from the saint's 1712 masterwork, *True Devotion to the Blessed Virgin Mary,* in the Apostolic Letter of Pope John Paul II, *Rosarium Virginis Mariae* (2002), n. 15.

painful effects of two unnecessary surgeries. She offered the pains and humiliations of her condition to Our Lady as atonement for sinners. One day when her mother asked her to drink some milk because of her extremely fragile condition she refused. Her mother thought she was being obstinate, but actually the very act of drinking caused the child extreme pain. Lucia later reproached her for being disobedient to her mother and Jacinta then agreed to drink the milk, which she found agonizing and nauseating. Later she told Lucia: "I drink it all for love of Our Lord and of the Immaculate Heart of Mary, our dear heavenly Mother." She then added, "I have such pains in my chest! But I don't say anything. I'm suffering for the conversion of sinners."[163] This wisdom came from the mouth of a nine-year-old child.

FOUNDATION STONES OF A
SERIOUS FATIMA SPIRITUALITY IN OUR LIVES

A certain formula for union with Our Lady's intentions was prescribed by Our Lady of Fatima Herself. It has three essential elements which are the foundation stones of a serious Fatima spirituality: 1.) the Rosary 2.) the Scapular, and 3.) the Five First Saturdays for reparation. Among all the possible Marian devotions, why these three? The short answer to this question is that *Our Lady asked for these.* In each of the six apparitions of 1917 She told the children to pray the Rosary and to encourage others to constantly pray the Rosary. Concerning the dignity and efficacy of the Rosary, Pope Leo XIII pointed out that

> the origin of this form of prayer is divine rather than human, showing it to be an admirable garland woven from the Angelic Salutation, together with the Lord's Prayer, joined to meditation, and that this form of prayer was most powerful and particularly efficacious for attaining eternal life. For besides the special excellence of the prayers, it affords a powerful protection to faith and conspicuous models of virtue in the mysteries proposed for contemplation.[164]

I believe that the value of the Rosary as a spiritual force uniting us to

---

163   Haffert, *Her Own Words*, 48.

164   Pope Leo XIII, Encyclical Letter on the Rosary, *Diurni Temporis* (1898), n. 4.

Our Lady and to Our Lord needs very little comment. Its power is well-attested to in the history of the Church and in the experience of the faithful. Likewise, the appearance of Our Lady of Mt. Carmel holding the Scapular in the October 1917 apparition should also be evidence enough that the wearing of the brown Scapular is an integral part of the Fatima devotion. Sr. Lucia told Mr. Haffert that Our Lady "wants everyone to wear it. It is, as Pope Pius XII has said, the sign of consecration to Her Immaculate Heart." When he asked for a clarification of which of the two devotions was more important, Sr. Lucia said that "the Scapular and the Rosary are inseparable."[165] These two devotions, united as one, should be the clearest of all the elements of a Fatima spirituality; they come from the apparitions themselves.

The longer answer to the above question involves the other two foundation stones: the practice of the Five First Saturdays and the Daily Offering. With regard to the first, Our Lady made Her intentions and instructions clear to Sr. Lucia in a private apparition subsequent to the public apparitions of 1917. When Lucia was a novice with the Dorothean Sisters living at a convent in Pontevedra, Spain in 1925, Our Lady appeared to her and asked her to propagate the practice of the Five First Saturdays. Our Lady proposed this devotion to Sr. Lucia in the private apparition on December 10th of that year:

Look, my daughter, at my Heart, surrounded with the thorns with which ungrateful men pierce it at every moment with their blasphemies and ingratitude. You, at least, try to console me and announce that I promise to assist at the hour of death, with the graces necessary for salvation, all those who on the first Saturday of five consecutive months shall confess, receive Holy Communion, recite five decades of the Rosary, and keep me company for fifteen minutes while meditating on the fifteen mysteries of the Rosary, with the intention of making reparation to me.[166]

Here, Our Lady only clarified and expanded upon the public apparition of July 1917 where She cryptically mentioned that She would return to ask for the "communion of Reparation on the First Saturdays."

165   Haffert, *Dear Bishop*, 86; Haffert, *Sign of Her Heart*, 193.
166   Haffert, *Dear Bishop*, 225-26.

BUILDING UPON THE SOLID FOUNDATION:
THE REAL CHARISM OF THE PILGRIM VIRGIN STATUE

If we take to heart the message of Fatima and attempt to develop a serious Fatima spirituality, we will not be content to do the basics, although those devotions in themselves have plenty of sanctifying power. We will try to build upon the foundation that Our Lady has laid in our spiritual lives, and there are innumerable means by which to do so. Allow me to list a few of them, in no particular order, to emphasize how fully Our Lady and Her intentions may be integrated into the life of a believer:

- Consecrations: there are numerous forms of consecration to Our Lady, the most renowned of which is the Total Consecration laid out by St. Louis Marie de Montfort. While the Scapular in itself represents a consecration to Our Lady, the de Montfort consecration represents a development and deepening of this ancient practice.

- Marian teachings of the Popes: the body of doctrinal writings of the popes concerning Our Lady is an immense spiritual treasure that the Church offers to humanity;[167] it is said that more than fifty popes have written documents about Our Lady and one pope in particular, Pope Leo XIII, published eighteen separate writings on the Rosary.[168] Clearly, there is no lack of insight in Church teachings about Our Lady's intentions for us and for the human race.

- Marian saints and martyrs: studying the example of the greatest Marian saints is the best way to develop a serious Fatima spirituality because the saints teach us how to give everything to Our Lady in union with the Church and according to the circumstances of our times;

- Marian devotional groups and movements: a final blessing to the

---

167   The website of the Vatican (www.vatican.va) lists at least fourteen mariological writings of popes of the recent centuries, from Papal Bulls and Apostolic Exhortations to full Marian encyclical letters.

168   Haffert, *Deadline,* 238.

Church are the many devotional groups and movements that offer people the chance to bond with other souls consecrated to Our Lady and Her wishes. Through these movements, the truths of our Faith are more deeply implanted in our hearts, and we develop a solidarity with the "Marian church" of souls dedicated to Her plan of sanctification. It is particularly important to remain united with priests who have the charism of preaching, teaching, and witnessing to Our Lady in the modern day as well as with groups that carry out the mission of mercy for souls according to Our Lady's wishes.

THE TRIUMPH OF HER IMMACULATE HEART BEGINS WITH EACH OF US

I am convinced that we will not understand how Our Lady intends to bring about the ultimate Triumph of Her Immaculate Heart for the world unless each of us begins to recognize Her smaller victories in our own lives. By this I mean that we must experience and be open to the potency of Her grace in action around us and the immense rewards of our personal dedication to Her Fatima message. Through Her Immaculate Heart we ask Our Lord to grant us the depth of radical faith that will be needed to usher in the universal victory of Her Heart. That is a prayer that Jesus will not fail to answer, for, as we mentioned at the beginning of this chapter, it was Jesus's Will to establish devotion to His Mother's Immaculate Heart in the first place.

As a final word, I would like to offer some concrete possibilities to the reader about how we may "apply" a serious Fatima spirituality to the problems and sins of our world, and indeed to the many difficult circumstances of our own lives. A devout person can experience the Triumph of the Immaculate Heart in so many ways:

- By asking Our Lady's intercession to overcome a habitual personal sin or addiction;
- By turning to Her in any crisis situation, personal or familial;
- By commending a spiritually "lost" family member, friend, or even someone unknown to Her Immaculate Heart;

- By making a pilgrimage of reparation to a Marian shrine;
- By joining the pro-life cause in an integral way; Our Lady's desire to save the unborn from destruction and the abortionists from sin is primary in this day and age;
- By learning to trust and confide all things to Her, both our long-term problems and our short-term goals and plans.

Our Lady loves us so much! We cannot fathom the depth of Her love for humanity as a whole and for each one of us in particular. She sees every single person on the face of the earth as Her own special child and wishes only that we will choose to live with Christ Her Son for all eternity. Nothing would please Her maternal Heart more than to have us with Her in the Kingdom of Christ. That call is what the Pilgrim Virgin Statue has been issuing for the past seventy years. Wherever She has traveled She has invited the faithful, through her captivating and consoling maternal gaze, to come to Her and to experience Her personal and tender love for them.

Let us have confidence in Our Lady *in all things*! Let us believe with all our hearts that She is watching over us and seeks to transform all the circumstances of our lives, painful or joyful, into victory. Let us not despair of any sin or its effects, or cower at the enormity of the many structures of sin all around us. The Woman who made the sun dance in the sky in October of 1917 is the same one who has asked us to remain close to Her Immaculate Heart. She holds the world in Her Heart, and together with Her, we offer that world and all its outrages, sacrileges, and indifference together with our unique sufferings, asking for His Divine Mercy to flow down upon us through the hands of the Lady who is so holy that She is "clothed with the sun" (cf. Rev 12:1-3).

With Our Lady of Fatima, we have nothing to fear. With Her we can be confident that everything, absolutely everything in our lives, will work out alright. As Our Lady prophetically stated in the message of Fatima, "Finally, in the end, my Immaculate Heart with triumph."

Conclusion

THE CELESTIAL HERALD OF PEACE AND HOPE

*O Mary, into your maternal hands I place myself and I abandon
myself completely, sure of obtaining whatever I ask of you. I trust in you
because you are the sweet Mother, I confide in you because you are the Mother
of Jesus. In this trust I place myself, sure of being heard in everything; with
this trust in my heart I greet you "my Mother, my trust," I devote myself
entirely to you, begging you to remember that I am yours, that I belong
to you; keep me and defend me, O sweet Mary, and in every instant
of my life, present me to your Son, Jesus.[169]*
~St. Gianna Beretta Molla, 1922-1962.

*I*n my travels with the International Pilgrim Virgin Statue over the
course of some thirty-five years, I have witnessed with astonishment,
many signs of a *moral resurrection* in the souls of countless people
who have visited the Statue. I have felt a rebirth of their hopes for a virtuous
life and the victory of purity in lives where unbridled decadence had previously ruled. I saw people devastated by adversity who had found in devotion
to Our Lady an oasis of peace and relief. I saw them discover, as I had, the
dominant and radiating characteristics of Our Lady's most pure soul: Peace
and Hope. The Litany of Loreto calls Her by the title of Queen of Peace, and
Pope Pius XII named Her the "Mediatrix of peace,"[170] one of the most beautiful descriptions of Her heavenly mission that I have ever heard.

Our Lady is undoubtedly a messenger of the peace of Heaven to everyone who comes into contact with Her, and She is perhaps the last and best

---

169 *Reflections of St. Gianna Beretta Molla*, https://saintgianna.org/reflectionosst.htm.

170 Pope Pius XII, Encyclical Letter, *Ad Caeli Reginam* (1954), n. 51.

hope of peace for our sad world. But is this just a pious message for the already-devout, or a bit of moral naiveté that is incapable of resolving the serious problems that our world faces? Not at all. Allow me to address this question with a story.

THE POWERFUL EFFECTS OF
THE FATIMA MESSAGE: THE JESUITS OF HIROSHIMA

The only time in history when an atomic bomb was deployed in actual warfare was at the end of the Second World War. In fact, it was the dropping of the dual atomic bombs on Hiroshima and Nagasaki, Japan on August 6th and 9th, 1945 respectively that ended the War. More importantly, it was a war that *could have been avoided* if people had listened to Our Lady of Fatima's message. But even though the leaders of our nations ignored Our Lady's message and plunged the world into a senseless war hardly twenty years after the apparitions, the fact remains that *some people* at that time did in fact take the message of Fatima to heart.

At 8:17 on the fateful morning of August 6th, 1945 the entire center of Hiroshima was wiped out by the blast of the first nuclear bomb that eradicated everything within a mile radius of the epicenter. A radius of three miles was ravaged by a further wave of death and destruction, and virtually all buildings as far away as six miles from the bomb's epicenter were damaged. The Catholic Church of Our Lady's Assumption was within the immediate blast radius of one mile, and the eight Jesuit priests who were assigned to the parish were either in the church or in the rectory at the moment of the blast. The parish priest, German Jesuit Fr. Hubert Schiffer, had just finished celebrating Mass and was sitting down to his breakfast when he noticed the immense flash of light from the bomb. "Suddenly," he said, "a terrific explosion filled the air with one bursting thunder stroke. An invisible force lifted me from the chair, hurled me through the air, shook me, battered me, whirled me 'round and round' like a leaf in a gust of autumn wind." A number of the eight priests who were housed at that parish suffered physical injuries as a result of the impact of the bomb, but not one of them suffered the after-effects of radiation at any time thereafter, the effects of which killed hundreds of thousands. "We survived because we were living the message of Fatima," explained Fr. Schiffer. "We lived and prayed the Rosary daily in that home."[171]

THE POWER OF MARIAN CONSECRATION AND PRAYER

The lover of Our Lady of Fatima has no difficulty in interpreting those events. An atomic bomb is the harnessed power of a nuclear reaction; it is fire from heaven and a smaller version of what the earth's sun produces continuously from ninety-three million miles away. When such awesome power was used as a weapon, it rained down instant annihilation upon 80,000 people from the sky. The lingering effects of the radiation poisoning brought death to more than 300,000 people within the next few months. The world reeled in shock and disgust at the magnitude of such a horror never before witnessed in the history of humanity.

Yet, this single greatest destructive power known to man proved to be virtually incapable of inflicting any long-term harm on the consecrated men who lived their lives in union with Our Lady of Fatima and Her message. Those eight priests experienced their own Miracle of the Sun that day and, like the 70,000 witnesses in October 1917, they lived to tell the story of the radiant Lady whose glory outshines even the sun's light and force. The Book of Revelation describes Our heavenly Lady as a "woman clothed with the sun" and Her appearance as a "great sign" (Rev 12:1). If the nullification of the power of a nuclear weapon is not a great and heavenly sign of God's protection, then nothing is.

Cardinal Ratzinger, in the 2000 Vatican statement on Fatima, made a striking observation: "Today the prospect that the world might be reduced to ashes by a sea of fire no longer seems pure fantasy: man himself, with his inventions, has forged the flaming sword."[172] The truth of that statement should sober every rational person. In the face of that power, a greater weapon is needed, a protective shield to counteract the self-destructive urge

171   Myra Adam, "A Divine Miracle for Skeptics Who Do Not Believe in Miracles," *PJ Media*, 6/24/12; http://pjmedia.com/lifestyle/2012/06/24/a-divine-miracle-for-skeptics-who-do-not-believe-in-miracles/?singlepage=true.

172   Congregation for the Doctrine of the Faith, The Message of Fatima, Theological Commentary, 6/26/00.

of mankind. The message of Fatima leaves no room for equivocation. Repentance, atonement for sin, personal moral conversion, and a heartfelt return to God are the answer to the evils of our day.

The foundation stones of prayer and consecration that we laid out in the last chapter are the tangible means by which we join Our Lady in averting this kind of annihilation and human self-destruction. She doesn't ask us to perform heroic acts of self-sacrifice or impossible feats of piety. She simply asks us to intensify our spiritual exercises. As John Haffert noted more than once, this is a *spiritual* battle, and one that will only be won "on our knees."[173] The Fatima message is not yesterday's concern. Both the Hiroshima incident and the many other stories that I have recounted in these pages show that it is a message for today, and it is a message of great hope in the midst of a world full of death and despair.

A SACRAMENTAL SIGN FOR THE WORLD

The International Pilgrim Virgin Statue is a tangible reminder of the message of Fatima, perhaps the most beautiful legacy of Our Lady's intervention in recent history. I have been so privileged to accompany this marvelous *sacramental sign* of Our Lady's presence to various nations of the world, a gift that I consider to be one of the foremost blessings I have ever received. I know that I was called to this task long ago, and I have tried to offer the many sacrifices of my life and my travels in union with Her intentions; but I feel as though there is always more that She calls me to do for the advancement of Her peace plan. I pray that this book, witnessing to the many wonders of the Pilgrim Virgin Statue, will be pleasing to Our Lady and to Our Lord and will bring many souls into His Kingdom of grace and peace.

The message of Fatima is a warning of utmost seriousness to an age that has rejected and offended God in countless ways. We simply cannot ignore Our Lady's pleas for conversion and expect to escape the consequences that sin draws down upon us. Like Moses at the end of his life, when he laid out the stark "life or death" choice facing the people of Israel (Dt 30:15-19), Our Lady clearly stated what the consequences would be for obedience to Her

173   Haffert, *Russia Converted*, 144.

message – or for its rejection: "If my requests are heeded, Russia will be converted, and there will be peace. If not, she will spread her errors throughout the world…."[174] Sr. Lucia said that "in His kindness, God warns and calls us to the right path, respecting the freedom He has given us."[175] We have the freedom to respond in faith to Her requests.

After remaining so close to the Pilgrim Virgin Statue for so many years, however, I am convinced that warnings of doom and destruction are the *penultimate*, not the final, word of Our Lady of Fatima. She warns us because She loves us! Her love is the ultimate reality and the sole reason for Her intervention into the affairs of the human race. A mother exhorts and admonishes, even scolds when necessary, out of the abundance of love that She bears toward a child who is in danger of being hurt by his own folly. Yet, would anyone say that harsh, protective words are the only signs of a mother's love toward the child of her womb? Mothers must warn their children of impending doom, but a mother's love is also an ocean of tender mercy for the child who listens to her plea.

Our Lady of Fatima's way of appealing to Her children – so evident in the magnetic effect of the Pilgrim Virgin Statue – is the way of attraction, of beauty, and of heartfelt love that communicates itself through peace of heart. The International Pilgrim Virgin Statue has been a messenger of hope for the world since José Thedim created his magnificent and blessed sculpture in 1947. There was truly something of divine inspiration in his creation. So many millions of people who have come into contact with the Statue throughout seventy years of Her travels have experienced the profound peace and certain hope that attends Her like the train of a bejeweled robe trails behind the presence of a queen. To this day healings, miracles, and astounding transformations take place when souls open their hearts to Her beauty and message. Each of us has an interior space in our souls for a Mother who never gives up on us for any reason. She has promised that "in the end" She will be victorious over the sins of humanity, but in order for that promise to be fulfilled She needs open ears, willing hearts, and generous souls.

174   Haffert, *Her Own Words*, 255.

175   Sr. Lucia's 1982 letter to Pope John Paul II, cited in Congregation for the Doctrine of the Faith, *The Message of Fatima*, Theological Commentary, 6/26/00.

With that in mind, I'd like to offer a final witness about the Pilgrim Virgin Statue to our readers. In 2011 Fr. Anthony Blatt invited Carl Malburg to bring the Pilgrim Virgin to his parish in the Diocese of Steubenville, Ohio.[176] The visit became an occasion for him to tell Mr. Malburg about the remarkable intervention the Pilgrim Virgin Statue of Our Lady of Fatima had made in his life some twenty years earlier. Father's touching story is one of the many incredible victories of Our Lady's Immaculate Heart that we have presented in this book, but it is also a fitting witness with which to end because it involves one of Our Lady's special priest sons who, because of his unique calling as a priest of God, has multiplied the graces of Our Lady for others.

> In my youth I had wandered away from the faith for a long time, but for the very first time in many years I felt like going back to church. It was probably out of curiosity when I heard about the miraculous statue coming to my small town. I did not really know what magnetized me to come to see the statue of Our Lady of Fatima, but there is one thing I know for sure: it was the beginning of my new life. It was Our Lady who directed me to a life of faith and hope in Her Son. It may have taken some years of discernment and seminary formation, but certainly it was the hand of God through the intercession of Mary which enabled me to respond to this calling. There is always a specific time when God calls each of us. This specific visit of the International Pilgrim Virgin Statue was no doubt the occasion of my lifelong conversion and onward to a priestly vocation. I owe my priesthood first to God, then to Our Lady of Fatima.

We too, each in our own way, are ministers of the life-saving message of Our Lady of Fatima. We have only to offer ourselves to Her – and She will take care of the rest.

---

176   This lovely story is found in the *IPVS News,* Spring 2013 edition with slight editing for our presentation here.

MARY WE CROWN THEE WITH BLOSSOMS TODAY[177]

Mary, you are a Queen! The most Blessed Trinity has confidently placed the welfare of the Church into your powerful and gentle motherly hands, just as that same Church is entrusted to each of us at our Confirmation. You will lead the pilgrim people of God home to His infinite loving Heart. Giving you the Crown is a symbolic way to entrust to you once more the full responsibility for this task.

We wish to crown you because of our personal helplessness in facing the deep distress of our times. We struggle to find God and we search His inscrutable ways. We struggle with the distress of faith and the lack of it. Please join your blessed hands in prayer on our behalf. Tell your Divine Son as you once did at Cana of Galilee: "Lord, they have no wine!" Ask the Lord again and again to work miracles of peace, unity and prosperity for the poor and suffering.

Take our flowers for your Crown. Let them represent our wish to weave you a wreath of joy and thanksgiving for the coming era. Let us work with you, our sister in faith, to make this new millennium a Christ-centered age in which our people will do what He tells us! Be our Queen! Teach us what immense dignity there is in our Christian calling. Grant peace and joy to our hearts, grant peace and joy to our families.

---

177   Based on a prayer by St. Bernard of Clairvaux; cited in the *IPVS News*, Fall 2010 edition.

Lead our nation to follow paths of justice and assist each of us to be worthy to wear the crown of our calling that the Lord has prepared for us at the end of our journey. When we worry about our eternal salvation and the salvation of our family, friends and relatives, we will remember the Lord's promises fulfilled in Mary! When evil powers battle for our hearts and the hearts of our dear ones, we will remember the Lord's promises fulfilled in Mary!

And, Mary, when at last we may come home, when we face our good and mighty God to give an account of all our words and actions, we will remember Our Lord's promises fulfilled in you! We will rest secure in your motherly heart and proclaim with joy the greatness of the Lord as you have done.

Mary you are the joy of those in heaven, the help of those on earth, the consolation of those still burdened by their sins. Accept our May blossoms; accept each flower as a symbol of praise and thanksgiving! Thank you for your cooperation in the plan that changed the destiny of the world. Teach us, Mary; teach us that we too may make the place where we can become a little paradise for God. Mary, Mother and Queen, accept our crown!

Acknowledgements

In publishing this book on the cusp of the One Hundredth Anniversary of the apparitions of Our Lady of Fatima, I am aware of my profound debt to many individuals and organizations who are Her loyal sons and daughters. I would like to thank Mrs. Patricia Haffert above all, who has been both a personal friend and a valuable resource for information about her late husband, John Haffert, and the International Pilgrim Virgin Statue. No less valuable both for materials and for perspective were the numerous custodians of the Statue whom I have known over the years, particularly Mr. Carl Malburg and his wife Rose Mary, as well as Richard Fasanello, Louis Kaczmarek (now deceased), and the current Custodians, Patrick Sabat and Larry Maginot. We have all traveled with Our Lady's precious image and seen with our own eyes the wonders She performs around the world. There is no way to adequately thank God for such a grace, but I can thank each of these individuals publicly in this book for their gracious assistance in helping me to fulfill Mr. Haffert's wish.

I am particularly grateful to those individuals who put in many hours of reading, and (very charitably) critiquing the manuscript prior to its publication: my brother Michael McKenna, Dr. Antonio Borelli, Fr. Carl Gismondi, FSSP, and Brian Gail, as well as a few other individuals who have asked to remain anonymous. Their contributions have made this book a better gift to Our Lady, which is my fondest hope. Last of all but not least, I must thank my dear wife, Bridgette, for her loving and patient encouragement to me over these many years as I struggled with the burden of pulling all the materials together and making it into a book. I have been immensely blessed by her support.

The two organizations that have done more than any other groups to promote the Fatima message are the World Apostolate of Fatima (known previously as the Blue Army) and the worldwide network of Fatima apostolates of the Societies for The Defense of Tradition, Family, and Property (TFP). In the course of this book I have intended to give proper credit to the founders of these apostolates, Mr. John Haffert and Professor Plinio Corrêa de Oliveira, whose stories I presented in Chapter 4. I only pray that my words have been adequate to pay respect to the men who consecrated their lives so that the prophetic message of the Lady from Heaven would be better known to the world.

APPENDIX A
CUSTODIANS OF THE
INTERNATIONAL PILGRIM VIRGIN STATUE

Custodians	Dates of Custody
Msgr. William McGrath, SFM[178]	1947-1968
Fr. Joseph Breault, SFM and Fr. Gerard Breault, SFM	1970-1972
Fr. Sylvester Catallo, OFM, Cap.[179]	1972
Fr. Philip Higgins, CSC[180]	1973-1975
Society for the Defense of Tradition, Family, and Property (TFP-Brazil)	1975-1982
Mr. Louis Kaczmarek	1983-1992
Mr. Carl Malburg	1993-1996
Various Custodians in Oceania / Australia	1996-1997
Mr. Richard Fasanello	1998-1999
Mr. Carl Malburg (with Rose Mary Malburg)	1999-2014
Mr. Patrick Sabat (Co-Custodian/ sole Custodian)	2003-2014/2015-2016
Mr. Patrick Sabat and Mr. Larry Maginot (Co-Custodians)	2016 to the present

APPENDIX B
RESTORATIONS OF THE
INTERNATIONAL PILGRIM VIRGIN STATUE

As of the publication of this book, the Pilgrim Virgin Statue will have been on pilgrimages throughout the world for seventy years. Throughout its existence the Statue has traveled millions of miles encompassing the globe and

178   Scarboro Foreign Mission Society.

179   Order of Friars Minor, Capuchins.

180   Society of the Holy Cross.

has been venerated by tens of millions of faithful, if not more. Many have asked me how it is that She always looks so beautiful and well-preserved, and my first answer is that the extraordinary care the Custodians take with Her is a contributing factor. That being said, any material object, let alone a precious work of art that is exposed to everyday handling will eventually show signs of wear and tear over time. The simple fact of the breakdown of paint and finishes that occurs with age is inevitable. The primary factor of the Statue's preservation and ongoing radiance, however, has been the numerous restorations that She has undergone in Her seventy years.

THE FIRST TOTAL RESTORATION

The first general restoration was conducted over several months from 1977 to 1978 in Madrid, Spain. At the time, the Statue was in the care of the Society for the Defense of Tradition, Family and Property (TFP), and the pilgrimages were coordinated from Brazil. It was noted that the Statue was then entering its thirtieth year of constant pilgrimage and needed a thorough restoration. A member of the organization, Mr. Dias Tavares, was at that time a young, aspiring artist who would eventually become the official restorer of the Pilgrim Virgin Statue and a world-class artist in his own right. The restoration in the late Seventies was precipitated by a well-intended attempt in Chile during a pilgrimage to clean the face using an alcohol-based perfume, which resulted in its discoloration.

As Europe was known for the finest and most talented artists, Mr. Tavares was asked to be involved with the restoration of the Pilgrim Virgin which included interviewing artists who would have the adequate skills to carry out the work. The group went first to Rome where they interviewed a Vatican artist. Following that meeting they interviewed a renowned artist from Assisi who happened to be in Rome at the time.

With these interviews it became apparent that Italy was not the country with the leading polychrome artists but that Spain was considered the country where the best statue restorers were found due to their religious tradition and culture. Their research led them to the famous Prado Museum in Madrid where they consulted with the artists who restored the many valuable works of art on display there. They were eventually directed to the Solis brothers in Madrid, a team of three blood brothers who were quite well-known and worked together at the Museum of the Americas where they specialized in restoring works of art from Spanish American countries. Aside from their expertise, all three gentlemen were practicing Catholics and had a deep devotion to Our Lady.

The restoration took place over the course of several months, and the aspiring Dias Tavares was allowed to work with the brothers Solis to observe the restoration process. Over the course of those months he learned a great deal from the masters. Under their instructions he was given the duty of carefully removing the old paint from the entire Statue, a delicate task that required extreme care and a great deal of time. He explained to me that the task was to strip several coats of paint down to the layer that existed at the time when the statue was alleged to have cried tears in New Orleans in 1972. The most important and delicate work was therefore removing the paint on the face.

The brothers then proceeded with the re-painting, and the result of their meticulous craftsmanship was that the Statue was completely and perfectly restored. What was most noteworthy was that they achieved the restoration of the face while preserving the delicate and grace-filled physiognomy that is so significant to the Statue.

ADDITIONAL PARTIAL RESTORATION

In the Fall of 1981 the Statue was on pilgrimage in the United States when a crack appeared in the mantle due to an inexperienced assistant who inadvertently gripped it in a weak place. I had just returned from Canada with the Statue where I served on my first pilgrimage as Custodian. Subsequently, the Statue was returned to the Solis brothers in Spain for a very brief period to undertake this minor repair. It was in November of that year that I was asked if I would go to Spain to pick up the Statue and take it on the European tour that I detailed in Chapter 9. This was the year in which *"my travels with the Queen"* began.

THE SECOND COMPLETE RESTORATION

In the later part of the 1990's the Statue was on pilgrimage in Oceania for a period of about nine months and had several part-time Custodians traveling with Her, something that was unusual and is no longer permitted. The result of some untrained people handling the Statue was that Her hands had been broken and inadequately repaired. There had also been several failed attempts by amateur artists to touch up the face of the Statue which altered the delicate beauty of the face.

Providentially, Dias Tavares, who had been involved with the first general restoration, was now living in the United States and working with the TFP and their America Needs Fatima campaign. He had undertaken many different projects for them over the years. The Statue at the time was operating under the auspices of the Lay Apostolate Foundation and the custodianship of Carl Malburg and his wife Rose Mary. In coordination with all the above parties, we were able to arrange for Dias to carry out a complete restoration during the month of July, 1999. After he had completed the restoration Mr. Tavares shared with me something that both touched and inspired me. He said that restoring the Pilgrim Virgin had been *the dream of his life*. He stated that all his other works of art and paintings were simply preparing him for this moment and that he was extremely grateful for having been entrusted with that task.

The following is Dias Tavares' personal account of the restoration, and it is worth quoting in full.

MR. TAVARES' REPORT ON
THE RESTORATION OF THE PILGRIM VIRGIN STATUE

"First of all, I wish to say that I was able to perform a complete restoration of the Pilgrim Virgin Statue due to the efforts of Thomas McKenna who worked closely with the Custodians to arrange a time when I could work on the Statue for an extended period. Over the years the Statue had undergone several restorations (essentially alterations) by people who were not exactly skilled in the art of restoring statues.

"It was only possible to schedule one month for the restoration, which was carried out in July of 1999. My initial thought was to restore only the face, hands and feet so that the hands and feet matched the face. The face, of course, is the most important part of the Statue and was to be my primary focus. I knew that special attention had to be given to the eyes and the mouth which are the main features and elements that had been altered. I had in my mind to restore Our Lady to the way She was when I first saw Her in 1973. The challenge was to do all of this in the timeframe of one month! It was clear to me that finishing an optimal restoration in such a short time would be possible only with Divine intervention.

"When the Statue underwent restoration in 1977-78 in Spain, the artists had taken great care not to remove the layer of paint over which the tears flowed when the Statue was said to have cried in New Orleans in July of 1972. I feared that over the years the subsequent restorations would have removed this undercoat. However, much to my surprise, as I slowly removed at least three coats of paint with a scalpel, I found that the undercoat of paint on the Statue in 1972 was still intact. What aided me in restoring the Statue to its original state was the fact that I had numerous photos from the tears incident in 1972, which provided good references to guide me. I also had detailed photographs I had taken during the restoration of 1977-78, all of which proved to be very helpful.

"The golden border of the mantle was done with real gold leaf and was a very important element because it created the frame for the face. There are more modern methods of applying gold leaf, but these leave the finish very shiny, which looks inauthentic. So I resorted to the traditional method of gold leafing followed by the application of varnish. I also gold-plated the metal part of the Statue's base. Furthermore, the minor cracks and wear on the wooden mantle were covered with a special material for restoration that left it looking like new.

"When I began to paint the face, I strove to use oil paint and water colors in order to achieve the freshness and brilliance that the Statue had when I first saw it in 1973. I was very pleased with the results and to learn subsequently that Mr. John Haffert had expressed his great satisfaction and complete approval of the Statue's restoration when it was returned to him. Thomas McKenna recounted to me that upon seeing that newly restored Statue for the first time, Mr. Haffert approached to within inches of the face and gazed at it for a long time, before turning to everyone in the room and exclaiming in a jubilant smile, 'It is Our Lady – She is back! This is exactly how I remember the Statue. Thank you!'

"Since this restoration, there have been times when I performed other, minor, restorations and touch ups. One time her hands were broken again. Another time She fell and the head was damaged, but the face was never affected. To this day I have never had to repaint the face. I have worked retouching other parts of the Statue – the base, the mantle, the gold leafing, etc. – but never the face. These touch-ups are more like maintenance of the Statue because, with all of Her travels, it is natural that the Statue should experience the wear and tear of many miles and thousands of devotional touches."

JOSÉ THEDIM'S GIFT TO THE WORLD

One can only wonder what the original sculptor, José Ferreira Thedim, who died in 1971, would think of his masterpiece today. I'm sure he would marvel at the longevity and durability of the beloved Pilgrim Virgin who has travelled many more miles than any human missionary. He might be overawed at the crowds that consistently show up to view Her enchanting gaze and intense beauty anywhere in the world. He would undoubtedly experience that same sense of maternal love and attention that millions have personally witnessed over the years in Her presence and that only seems to accumulate in grace and intensity the more She travels. He would be immensely grateful to the numerous faithful Custodians and to the talented restorers who have treated one of the Church's greatest sacramentals with profound reverence and who have continually made Her available to as many as wish to pray before Her and listen to the message of Fatima.

I believe that Our Lady smiles on José Thedim's loveliest creation because the Pilgrim Virgin Statue never ceases to be a gift to the world.

Appendix C
On Pilgrimage Within a Gaze

By Plinio Corrêa de Oliveira[181]

A commentary on the miraculous
International Pilgrim Virgin Statue
of Our Lady of Fatima

I do not know a countenance equal to this one. Moved by an inveterate habit of observing everything, I contemplate it so that I may later understand it. As I fix my eyes upon that countenance, I suddenly perceive that I am entering it.

Yes, its unique expression emanates from the face and especially the eyes. Enveloped in the ambience it creates, I feel invited to enter deep into her gaze.

What a gaze! None other is so calm, frank, pure, or welcoming. In none other can one penetrate with such ease. None other holds such unfathomable depth or grand horizons. The more one penetrates this gaze, the more one is attracted toward an indescribable interior and sublime summit.

What summit? A state of soul I would be tempted to describe as full of paradoxes if the word "paradox," were not so misused today and thus appear disrespectful.

The Scholastics say every perfection results from the balance of harmonious opposites. Thus I am not speaking about a precarious balance between flagrant contradictions whereby our contemporary world seeks to maintain a poor stained and vacillating peace at the cost of so many shameful concessions. No, this is a supreme harmony of all forms of good.

In the depth of this gaze, I see arise precisely a peak where all perfections meet. It is a peak incomparably higher than the columns that support the firmament. It is a peak where a crystalline, categorical and irresistible rule excludes every form of evil, however slight or small.

One could spend a whole lifetime within that gaze, without ever reaching the summit of that peak. It is not however a useless effort. Within that gaze one does not walk, but flies. One is not a tourist but a pilgrim.

---

181   Plinio Corrêa de Oliveira, "Peregrinando dentro de um olhar", originally published in *Folha de São Paulo*, 11/12/76.

Although the pilgrim can never reach the height of that sacred mountain, the sum of all created perfection, he sees it with ever increasing clarity the more he flies toward her.

While on this pilgrimage of the soul, the pilgrim flies toward a gaze that does not merely envelope but penetrates him. Closing his eyes, he perceives a light in the depths of his being.

The gaze is the soul of the countenance. It is an impressive countenance! The fool might consider it inexpressive. To a skilled observer, it is greater than History because it touches eternity; greater than the universe because it reflects the infinite.

The forehead appears to contain thoughts that, beginning with a crib and ending with a Cross, take in all of human events.

The lines of the entire face and nose possess a charm "more beautiful than beauty." As a poet once wrote, these are silent lips that nevertheless say everything at every moment. They appear to praise God in the uniqueness of every creature, beseeching God to have pity on every pain and misery as if she had suffered from each one of them. These lips have an eloquence which reduces the orations of Demosthenes or Cicero to utter babble. What can be said of the skin other that it is snowy-white? This description says both everything and nothing. To describe it, one would need to imagine a snowiness that profoundly reflects with infinite discretion, all the shades of the rainbow, which would in turn inspire the soul that contemplated it with all the wonders of purity.

Yes, I went on pilgrimage within this gaze so filled with surprises. Yet, I unexpectedly feel that her gaze also went on pilgrimage inside me. Hers was a poor and merciful pilgrimage, not from splendor to splendor, but from need to need, from misery to misery. If only I open myself to her, she will offer me a remedy for my shortcomings, help against every obstacle and hope for every affliction.

This statue is a wooden statue without any special artistic value like so many others. And yet, one only has to fix one's eyes on this statue to see that, without moving or the least physical transformation, it becomes brilliant with all these splendors.

I do not know how this happens. However, if the reader wishes, let him look and see... I insist. If you believe in the description that I have made, I invite you in turn to make this magnificent pilgrimage within the gazes of the Virgin. If you do not believe, look and see. I could not offer a better invitation...

I pray to her for thee. I pray for the Holy Church troubled and tormented as never before.

BIBLIOGRAPHY

Apostoli, C.F.R., Andrew. *Fatima for Today: The Urgent Marian Message of Hope*. San Francisco: Ignatius Press, 2010.

Borelli Machado, Antonio Augusto. *As Aparições e a Mensagem de Fátima Conforme os Manuscritos da Irmã Lúcia*. São Paulo: Artpress, 1996.

_____. *Fatima: Past or Future? The Unheeded Message*. Translated and Edited by Philip Moran. Glasgow: Tradition, Family, Property, 2005.

Corrêa de Oliveira, Plinio. *Revolution and Counter-Revolution*. York: American Society for the Defense of Tradition, Family and Property, 1993.

_____. "Pilgrimage within a Gaze." *Folha de São Paulo*. November 12, 1976.

_____. "Tears, a Miraculous Warning." *Folha de São Paulo*. August 6, 1972.

Durham, Michael S. *Miracles of Mary: Apparitions, Legends, and Miraculous Works of the Blessed Virgin Mary*. San Francisco: Harpercollings, 1995.

Esser, Ignatius. *The Fatima Week Sermons*. St. Meinrad: Grail Publication, n.d..

Fortin, Robert J., A.A. *The Catholic Chaplaincy in Moscow: A Short History*, 1934-1999. Brighton, Massachusetts: Assumptionist Fathers, 2004.

Haffert, John M. *Deadline: The Third Secret of Fatima*. Asbury: The 101 Foundation, Inc., 2001.

_____. *Dear Bishop! Memoirs of the Author Concerning the History of the Blue Army*. Washington, New Jersey: AMI International Press, 1982.

_____. *Her Own Words to the Nuclear Age: The Memoirs of Sr. Lucia*. Asbury: The 101 Foundation, Inc., 1993.

_____. *Queen's Promise*. Washington, New Jersey: Ave Maria Institute, 1966.

_____. *Russia Will Be Converted*. Washington, New Jersey: AMI International Press, 1954.

_____. *Sign of Her Heart*. Washington, New Jersey: Ave Maria Institute, 1971.

_____. *The Brother and I*. Washington, New Jersey: Ave Maria Institute, 1971.

_____. *The Day I Didn't Die*. Asbury: The 101 Foundation, Inc., 1998.

_____. *The World's Greatest Secret*. Washington, New Jersey: Ave Maria Institute, 1967.

_____. *There is Nothing More*. Washington, New Jersey: AMI Press, n.d.

_____. *To Shake the World: Life of John M. Haffert*. Asbury: The 101 Foundation, Inc., 2001.

_____. *Too Late?* Asbury: The 101 Foundation, Inc., 1999.

Johnston, Francis. *Fatima, the Great Sign*. Charlotte: Tan Books, 2012.

Kaczmarek, Louis. *The Wonders She Performs*. Manassas: Trinity Communications, 1986.

Kalvelage, Fr, Francis M., ed. *Kolbe: Saint of the Immaculate*. New Bedford: Franciscans of the Immaculate, 2001.

De Mattei, Roberto. *The Crusader of the 20th Century: Plinio Corrêa de Oliveira*. Herefordshire: Gracewing, 1998.

_____. *The Second Vatican Council (An Unwritten Story)*. Translated by Patrick T. Brannan, S.J., et al. Fitzwilliam: Loreto Publications, 2012.

McGrath, William C. *Fatima or World Suicide?* Ontario: The Scarboro Foreign Mission Society, 1951.

Paul VI. Apostolic Exhortation. *Signum Magnum*, 1967.

Pelletier, Joseph A. *The Sun Danced at Fatima*. New York: Image Doubleday, 1983.

Phillips, Andrea F, *Plinio: A Man for Our Times*. Spring Grove: American Society for the Defense of Tradition, Family and Property, 2010.

Pius XII. Encyclical Letter. *Ad Caeli Reginam*, 1954.

Dos Santos, Armando Alexandre. *As Aparições, a Mensagem e o Segredo de Fátima*. São Paulo: Artpress, 1999.

Socci, Antonio. *The Fourth Secret of Fatima*. Fitzwilliam: Loreto Publications, 2009.

Solimeo, Luiz Sérgio. *Fatima, a Message More Urgent than Ever*. The American Society for the Defense of Tradition, Family and Property, 2008.

Index

M

Maginot, Larry 187, 188

Magisterium 52

Malburg, Carl 48, 68, 69, 118, 147, 154, 160, 161, 184, 187, 188, 191

March for Life 134

Marian apparitions 13

Marian Congregation 50, 51

Marlburg, Rose Mary 118, 160, 187, 188, 191

Martins, S.J., Fr. Antonio 64

Marto, St. Francisco 14

Marto, St. Jacinta 14, 153, 173

Marxism 130

Masella, Cardinal Aloisio 29

Materialism 131

McGrath, SFM, Msgr. William C. 69, 70, 188, 198

McKenna, Thomas I, VII, 69, 151, 162, 187, 191, 193

Medellin, Colombia 149

Mediatrix of peace 179

Memoirs of Sr. Lucia 16, 197

Mendoza, Argentina 149

Merida, Venezuela 70, 149

Michelangelo of Portugal 28. *See also* José Thedim

Middle Ages 52

Miracle of the Doves 30

Miracle of the Sun 25, 74, 154, 181

Mitterand, Francois, President of France 132

Molla, St. Gianna Beretta 179

Montreal, Canada 139

Morocco 147, 148

Moscow, Russia 18, 36, 37, 38, 39, 41, 155, 197

Mother of the Church 75, 116, 154

Mother of the Clergy 154

Mozambique 148

Muslims 117, 148

Mystical Body of Christ (Antichrist) 129, 153

N

Nagasaki, Japan 180

National Shrine of Our Lady of Sorrows, Chicago 142

New Orleans, Louisiana 64, 190, 192

Niagara Falls, New York 78, 140, 141

North Korea 129

Northwest Airlines 126

Notre Dame University, Notre Dame, Indiana 142

O

O'Boyle, Cardinal Patrick 41

Oceania 145, 147, 188, 191

Odo of Cluny, St. 135

O'Hara, Bishop John 141, 142

O Legionário 51

Order of Friars Minor, Capuchins 188

Os Valinhos, Portugal 23

Ottawa, Canada 139, 140, 141

Our Lady of Akita 172

Our Lady of Czestochowa 113

Our Lady of Lapa 30

Our Lady of Mount Carmel 23, 25, 44

Our Lady of Sorrows 23, 25, 142

Our Lady of the Blessed Sacrament 163

P

Padre Pio, St. 113

Pakistan 116, 117

Pan Am Airlines 6, 10, 132

Paris, France 5, 49, 134, 135, 136

Peace Flights 116

Pelletier, Joseph A. 14, 198

Perillo, Captain Tom 124, 125

Philippines 146

Phillips, Andrea F. 3, 50, 53, 54, 198

Place de la Concorde, Paris 136

Pontevedra, Spain 175

Pope Benedict XVI 132, 167

Pope John Paul II 13, 65, 67, 115, 134, 148, 172, 173, 183